Electronic Voices

Contact with Another Dimension

Electronic Voices

Contact with Another Dimension

Anabela Cardoso

BOOKS

Winchester, UK
Washington, USA

First published by O-Books, 2010
O Books is an imprint of John Hunt Publishing Ltd., The Bothy, Deershot Lodge, Park Lane, Ropley,
Hants, SO24 0BE, UK
office1@o-books.net
www.o-books.com

For distributor details and how to order please visit the 'Ordering' section on our website.

Text copyright Anabela Cardoso 2010

ISBN: 978 1 84694 363 8

Design: Tom Davies

Printed in the UK by CPI Antony Rowe

We operate a distinctive and ethical publishing philosophy in all
areas of its business, from its global network of authors to
production and worldwide distribution.

Contents

Foreword

This is a remarkable book that should do much to further the cause of ITC (Instrumental Transcommunication) as an important area of psychical research. My own interest in ITC began nearly 40 years ago with the publication of Konstantin Raudive's book, *Breakthrough,* in which he detailed his extensive results using EVP (a form of ITC that captures apparently paranormal voices on audio tape). Raudive had become interested in ITC as a result of reading two books by Friedrich Jürgenson (*Voices from the Space* and *Radio Communications with the Dead*), renowned Swedish artist and documentary film-maker, in which he reported capturing what appeared to be paranormal voices not only on audio tape but actually during radio broadcasts. The fact that Jürgenson also produced results when tested under strictly controlled conditions by Professor Hans Bender, one of Europe's most respected psychical researchers, appeared to eliminate all apparent normal explanations, including the possibility that the voices were stray radio transmissions picked up accidentally and misinterpreted by listeners.

In 1989, my interest was further aroused by the late Samuel Alsop's book, *Whispers of Immortality,* in which, once again, impressive results at recording ostensibly paranormal voices on audio tape were reportedly obtained. Through the kindness of Samuel Alsop's daughter, Gillian, I subsequently obtained samples of the voices that she and her father had recorded, and on listening to them it was clear that the voices were not only clearly audible but on some occasions appeared to be addressed directly to the experimenters. I learnt from Gillian the identities of other British researchers obtaining significant results and I contacted two of the most successful, Gilbert Bonner and Raymond Cass, and both kindly sent me tapes of their results. In both cases there was no question of the reality of the voices and of the fact that they appeared to have been recorded under conditions that precluded normal explanations. None of the experimenters I contacted were interested in publicity or in financial reward; their concern was primarily with the light that ITC might shed on the survival of physical death.

In 1999, I was put in touch with Dr. Anabela Cardoso, and it is here that, in terms of my personal involvement, we come to the present book. I was informed that Anabela Cardoso was obtaining impressive results with her ITC experiments, and that she was anxious to work with scientists with a view to their checking her results and helping to take the work forward. I learned that she was not only an ITC researcher who spoke six languages and had a highly trained ear for discriminating human speech, she was also Portugal's senior woman diplomat who had served as Consul General in the USA, Spain and France, and in Japan and India where she had been the Portuguese Chargé d'Affaires. Her international reputation as a leading diplomat made it unlikely that she had taken up ITC research with a view to any personal gain. In fact, as I learned later, although sceptical herself, she had begun her research in an attempt to comfort a close friend who had lost her young son in a tragic boating accident and who was attempting to find some evidence of his survival.

As a consequence of my confidence in the serious nature of Anabela's work, in 2001 I accepted her invitation to be her guest in Lyon, where she had just taken up the post of Consul General. On the very first evening of my visit, Anabela took me into her studio where there was an array of five radios (two valve and three solid state), each tuned to a different point in between transmitting stations, so that the only sounds we could hear were radio static (Dr. Cardoso was using the Direct Radio Voice method, which she explains in detail in the book). In the course of our session with the radios, I heard clear and unmistakable voices coming through the radio static. Dr. Cardoso recorded the sounds using a good quality audio system, and when the session ended, we were able to play them back and confirm beyond doubt the presence of the voices, which were in Portuguese – Dr. Cardoso's first language – a language of which I have some knowledge.

Even for someone who has had a number of impressive experiences of psychic phenomena during my years of investigation with the Society for Psychical Research (SPR) and elsewhere, the results obtained that first evening far exceeded my expectations. The voices were clear, at normal volume, and beyond the possibility of any doubt. There was no sign of the faint, almost unintelligible voices obtained by some ITC experimenters. In addition, there was no doubt that the voices were direct communications with Anabela, and could not be dismissed as stray radio voices. Similarly impressive results were forthcoming on each day during the rest of my stay in Lyon.

In assessing the reality or otherwise of apparent psychic phenomena, there are two simple questions to be asked. Firstly, do the reported phenomena actually occur? And secondly, if they do occur can they be explained by normal means? If the answer to the first question is yes and the second question is no, then we have, ipso facto, a case for accepting their paranormality. Having established that the answer to the first of the above questions, when applied to Anabela's voices, was yes, I had to address the second question by searching for normal explanations. In answering this second question, one has, of course, to begin by establishing the integrity and reliability of the researcher or witness associated with the phenomena. As a psychologist with some experience in such matters, I had no doubt that in Anabela Cardoso's case integrity and reliability were beyond question. In addition, she had no reason to falsify results – indeed she was, in fact, hazarding a distinguished diplomatic career by publicly interesting herself in psychical research. It is a sad fact that, although psychical research addresses vital issues about the human mind and about profound matters such as survival of death, one invites the suspicion of professional colleagues by showing any involvement in the subject. Nowhere can this be truer than in the case of a high-profile career such as that of a diplomat. Dr. Cardoso was showing – and has continued to show – great professional and personal courage in her determination to undertake her ITC experiments and to make known her results.

However, although Anabela's integrity was in my view beyond question, as a researcher I still had to consider the possibility of subterfuge. There were two things that had to be investigated. Firstly, could the communications have been pre-recorded and played back by equipment hidden inside the radios? And secondly, could there be an accomplice somewhere in the house or grounds who was receiving transmissions of what was being said in the studio and who was transmitting responses? In answer to these questions, it should be said that Dr. Cardoso had only recently taken up her post in Lyon and was living in rented premises, and that as a busy diplomat with a highly responsible post (there are over 100,000 Portuguese resident in the area of France for which she had diplomatic responsibility) and had little opportunity to secretly set up the equipment needed to practice deception or to recruit suitable and sufficiently discreet accomplices. But in order to be sure, I used the complete freedom accorded to me as a guest to examine the house and grounds unaccompanied and in the necessary detail. The studio was open to me at all times of the day and night, and I inspected the equipment in the same detail. I had the same freedom on all of my subsequent visits and at no time over the four-year period covered by these visits did I find evidence of any kind to hint at, let alone support, the idea of fraudulent activity. The same was true when I visited Dr. Cardoso's residence in Vigo, Spain, where she also has a studio and where, once again, I was given complete freedom to carry out my investigations. On all grounds, I felt able to rule out the possibility of pre-recording or of accomplices.

I also decided on a simple but potentially effective test of the voices. Without informing Anabela I had this test in mind; I requested the communicator to repeat a short phrase after me, namely 'Hello David'. The communicator did as I requested, and full details of this successful test, which are on audio tape, are given in the book. Later, I repeated this experiment in the studio in Vigo this time using the phrase 'How are you?' and once more without any prior warning. Again, on request, I received a clear and unequivocal repetition of the phrase (full details of this test are also given in the book).

After working with Anabela Cardoso on my many visits to her studios in Lyon and in Vigo, my conclusions can be simply stated. Firstly, I have no doubt about the reality of the voices received, and secondly, I am confident that these voices are not susceptible to normal explanation. Furthermore, as Anabela explains in the book, acoustic analysis of the voices appears to indicate that they lack characteristics present in the human voice, which further supports the view that they are not manmade. This being so, from where do the voices come? The only evidence we have is what the voices tell us themselves. Over and over again they insist that they 'are the dead', and provide us with descriptions of their world that accord with descriptions of the afterlife given to us through mediums. It could be argued that the voices set out deliberately to mislead us, but the information that Dr. Cardoso gives in the book indicates that this is extremely unlikely, and even if it were true it fails to explain the origin of the voices. Some commentators suggest that they might be from extra-terrestrials (UFOs have been suggested) but this not only leaves unanswered the question regarding why they should wish to deceive us, it also leaves us wondering why we should prefer an explanation involving extra-terrestrials, for whose existence there is no evidence, over an explanation involving survival of death, a possibility for which psychical research has built up some impressive evidence. Ultimately, the reader must study the details given in this book and make up his or her own mind.

Many years ago, Sir William Crookes, one of the UK's great scientists, whose own experimental research convinced him of the reality of psychic phenomena, answered critics who protested that the experiences he was describing were not possible with the words, 'I do not say it is possible; I say that it happened.' Crookes recognized that to protest that something is not possible, because we have no theory to explain it, is not good science. If many of the men and women who have furthered our scientific understanding had decided in advance that something was not possible we would never have had a Galileo or a Copernicus or a Newton or a Darwin or modern quantum physics. The starting point of good science is observation. In the course of this observation, phenomena sometimes occur that do not fit in with prevailing theoretical models, but this does not mean that the phenomena have not happened. It means that the prevailing models either have to be amended, discarded, or set aside as inappropriate to explain the new discoveries. Science progresses by seeing what is there, not by turning a blind eye to it.

We have a long way to go before ITC is more clearly understood. Like all psychic phenomena, it can at times be unpredictable in occurrence and subject to many variables that we (and it seems the communicators themselves) do not understand. But one thing is clear; Dr. Cardoso's work is an outstanding example of meticulous, committed investigative research. She has devoted many years of her life to this research, and has produced results of great interest to those people who value good psychical research, as well as to those people who seek to answer questions about non-material realities and man's possible survival of physical death.

One of the great advantages of ITC is that the phenomena are objective. Potentially all who are present during the experiments can hear the voices. Equally importantly, they can examine the equipment to satisfy themselves that there are no suspicious circumstances. In addition, when on audio tape or digital recorder, the voices can be treated as a PPO (a Permanent Paranormal Object) for the purposes of acoustic analysis designed to establish how the voice characteristics compare with the human voice and with (if available) tapes of the supposed communicator made during his or her physical life.

ITC, thus, has many advantages for the study of the hypothesis of survival of physical death, and it is now reportedly being widely investigated by researchers in continental Europe (some of whom Anabela and I have visited with the help of a generous grant from the late Oliver Knowles in order to record their results) and in the USA. Currently ITC is less well known in the UK and the appearance of this book will, I hope, do much to remedy this state of affairs. The book is, in fact, a major landmark not only in the investigation of ITC but in the history of psychical research and I wish it every success. Dr. Cardoso has done us a great service not only by the countless hours she has spent in her laborious and time-consuming research, but by sharing her results with us in such an accessible and illuminating way.

Professor David Fontana

Former President of the Society for Psychical Research

Introduction

The story I shall tell is a true personal story that happened to a normal person. This book describes amazing and unexpected events that suddenly and deeply transformed my life. All facts, situations and names reported are correct and are dealt with accurately. It is also an extraordinary story of love; a story that speaks of rare things that some will deem impossible.

We are so used to considering that this or that does not exist, that certain things cannot happen – for the simple reason that there are no laws to explain them – and suddenly we find ourselves suspended as if floating in an unknown space; although in a strange way our feet are as much on the ground as before. This is what happens when something we had previously regarded as 'impossible' happens in our lives.

The reference points of a lifetime fade away; mental patterns on which we have based the construction of our reality are irremediably shaken without obvious substitutes. Part of our identity, that important part that enables us to view the world in a conventional and traditional way like everybody else, crumbles into pieces. Many of the guidelines given to us by our education and our social and cultural milieu disappear, along with some of the values that have informed our lives from our early years. In their place a much expanded view of life arises in which habitual mental frontiers no longer have a place.

The telling of this story is necessary for many reasons, the most important of which is that a similar story can happen to anyone. The marvelous and indeed astounding events involved may vary, but at the core will always be the same experience of a shifting of the boundaries of what is considered possible and impossible. The reader will also find in my story a description of what has now come to be called Instrumental Transcommunication (ITC), a modern method through which amazing contacts with beings in an unseen domain of reality, that many call 'the other world' (and I prefer to call the next world), have been obtained. Instrumental Transcommunication has 50 years of systematic study and research behind it, but it has already opened up a path of such richness that many of the results obtained by means of it provide us with some of the most objective and impressive proof yet obtained that life does not finish with the death of the physical body.

The book also includes a brief description of the men and women who have pioneered ITC work, as well as a summary of the results achieved by contemporary researchers. My personal experiences and experimental methods are described in great detail, together with descriptions of the electronic equipment I have used from the outset and of the contacts that have been developed with the next world during the course of my work. I am in no doubt that the precise nature of the equipment used is not critical to the success of the communications received, yet once the initial contacts have been established the nature and quality of this equipment can facilitate the quality with which the voices of the communicators are heard, and can help with the analysis and comprehension of the messages involved. Thus, they do play a vital role in improving this electronically mediated contact with an unknown dimension from where our apparently deceased loved ones, both human and animal, insist on telling us that they continue (I quote from one of my own communications) to live in 'a world very similar to yours [our own] but much more beautiful' (translation from the original in Portuguese).

It may be that the electronic devices we are now using represent only a drop in an immense ocean of probabilities – the majority of which are unknown to us – that combine with each other to make the contacts possible. One of the goals of this book will be to contribute to a better understanding of these probabilities in order to further our comprehension of the processes that facilitate the contacts. Another goal is to help readers to try for themselves these electronic means of communication with the next world. No intermediaries, such as mediums, and no 'special conditions' – as the communicators themselves have said – are necessary. If possible, and at the risk of appearing presumptuous, I would also like to think that the book may contribute to an awakening of interest among the scientific community in the vital study and analysis of the objective and repeatable phenomena concerned, using the sophisticated technical methods of voice and image analysis that are fortunately now available to us.

This is a book written with the heart but fashioned in the most objective, rigorous and clear way of which I am capable. All facts reported are real and are described in an accurate and precise manner. Nothing has been omitted, and nothing has been added to my account of the extraordinary events that have transformed my life from that day on the 17th of January 1998 when the Portuguese word 'Sim' (yes) unaccountably appeared to have been recorded on the audio tape I was using in reply to the question I had just addressed to the inhabitants of a shadowy world, about whose existence at that time I had no certainties and had instead many doubts.

I have tried, in the book, to convey to the reader without exaggeration the process of deep transformation and of consciousness expansion that this extraordinary life experience has brought about in me. My purpose is above all to offer relevant information in a plain and unbiased way. My hope is that, by sharing experiences that I consider overwhelming in their transcendence and yet simplicity, I will encourage readers to try to embark upon similar marvelous adventures. As one of my main communicators, who called himself Carlos de Almeida, said to me one day – apparently from the next world – 'It is for humble people; it is to call upon love, [the] panacea of the world. It would be beautiful would it not?'

Chapter 1

What is ITC?

Definitions and Meanings

Instrumental Transcommunication (ITC) is an area of psychical research that has captured the attention of many thousands of people all over the world, particularly in the last couple of decades. Yet, surprisingly, many people have still not heard of it. The term itself – Instrumental Transcommunication – will puzzle many readers. It can literally be understood as 'communication beyond' or 'further than [normal] communication', with the word 'instrumental' referring to the involvement of electronic devices. ITC is therefore an electronically mediated form of communication with something (apparently the next dimension of existence) beyond the known reality.

The term was coined by Dr. Ernst Senkowski (1989), a retired Professor of Physics at the Technical University of Bingen in Mainz, Germany, and one of the most eminent figures in the international field of ITC research. Dr. Senkowski's book, *Instrumentelle Transkommunikation*, is the standard and best researched text on the subject currently available, containing an extensive range of precise and detailed information covering almost 40 years of the subject's growth and development since the pioneering work of the outstanding Swedish artist and documentary film maker, Friedrich Jürgenson.

The human longing to discover if there is something beyond physical death has been with us since the dawn of recorded history, and there are many indications that it was also in men's minds even in prehistoric days. Dr. Hernani Guimarães Andrade from Brazil, a leading investigator of all forms of psychical phenomena and in particular of those relating to survival of physical death, in his *A Transcomunicação Através dos Tempos*, gives a particularly comprehensive account of the various attempts made by humans across the centuries to contact a possible dimension of life beyond death. Abundant evidence pointing to the reality of this dimension has also been put forward by the many rigorous and methodical studies carried out by eminent researchers, such as Ernesto Bozzano, Camille Flammarion, William Crookes, Oliver Lodge, Alan Gauld, David Fontana, François Brune, Nils-Olof Jacobson and many others.

It is not the aim of this book to review the range of evidence concerned (see Fontana 2005 for a recent comprehensive survey), as my main concern is with that yielded over the last half century by ITC communications, but I would like to make it clear that ITC contacts seem to represent the continuation and, to some extent, the culmination of the endeavors carried out by communicators throughout the centuries to convey to us the simple and fundamental message that life continues beyond physical death in another domain of reality.

What kind of evidence is provided by ITC?

The basic evidence for survival provided by ITC takes the form of voices, images and texts recorded on electronic media by methods still inexplicable by modern science. I shall deal principally with the contacts provided through voices, as my own research focuses chiefly on this area, and my most important results have been produced through this medium. These voices, most of which sound to the ear like human voices, are received on magnetic tapes or digital recorders using a method commonly called EVP (Electronic Voice Phenomena) or VOT (Voices on Tapes). Alternatively, they emanate spontaneously from the loudspeaker of a radio (known as the DRV or Direct Radio Voices method), usually in response to questions or comments by the human experimenter. Both VOT and DRV voices are supposedly produced by invisible communicators who for the most part identify themselves as deceased humans. The messages received by both means, but mainly by the DRV that allow for in some cases lengthy dialogues, cover a large spectrum of information, some of it previously unknown to the experimenter, from the identification of the communicator and other deceased individuals, to detailed descriptions of the next world, and to high ethical teachings.

ITC voices usually manifest in response to contact attempts by live human investigators, although the first known recordings of such voices that we have on record appeared spontaneously on the wire recording devices that preceded the modern tape recorder. The recipients were two very eminent Catholic priests and academics who had no thought of trying to contact the Beyond, and were, in fact, working with Gregorian chants. Since these initial contacts, ITC communications have rapidly become well established, and are currently producing an extensive range of impressive evidence on survival, providing us with highly significant psychical phenomena of great value in its own right, quite apart from its relevance to survival.

Methods used by apparent communicators from the other world in the past were all appropriate to the epochs concerned, and the same is now true of ITC. ITC is, in fact, entirely adapted to the technology of our time, in view of the fact that, since communications were first received on planet Earth in a systematic way, in the spring of 1959 by Friedrich Jürgenson, our civilization has quickly evolved into a technological society based principally upon electronics.

Communications that I have received in the course of my own research, and that I will describe in more detail later in the book, tell us that 'There is another world. There is another way'; and it seems that in our era, the medium they have chosen through which to give us details of this other world is chiefly ITC, which uses the means and the language that characterize our modern world, namely the electronic media to which a large and ever-growing majority of the world population have access in one form or another.

The evidence provided through ITC appears to originate not only in the minds of invisible communicators but of invisible communicators who apparently can listen to (or receive in some way) the questions and comments made by the human experimenters who seek to work with them. Moreover, the results are available for examination by all those with sufficient interest in the subject. These results, therefore, represent what is sometimes referred to as the Holy Grail of psychical research, namely a Permanent Paranormal Object (PPO), i.e. an object that is not transient and fleeting as are most of the so-called 'paranormal' phenomena, but that remains accessible to detailed testing and examination by believers and skeptics alike.

A Brief Guide to ITC Terms and Methodology

This is a convenient point at which to pause and explain some of the terms used in this book, together, where appropriate, with a brief introduction to the research methods associated with them.

Firstly, the word 'paranormal': Despite the fact that this is still the most widely used and recognizable description for any form of any psychic phenomena, it is in my view inappropriate in that it distances these phenomena from our normal world. In consequence, I shall use the term 'anomalous' instead. There is nothing really 'paranormal' in life. For example, electromagnetic waves, quantum events, black holes, etc. are invisible to the naked eye and in many instances follow laws that contradict those of the rest of physical science, yet we do not regard them as 'paranormal', even though, for many centuries, there was no clue to their existence. Everything is, in fact, natural, no matter how unusual, rare, unknown or invisible it is. Everything belongs to Life or Nature; the mysterious, amazing force that brings plants, minerals and animals into being. Thus, the term 'anomalous' seems more appropriate, since it simply means out of or beyond the norm. There are other expressions used in the parapsychological literature that I do not agree with and I shall inform the reader of them when the occasion arises.

Secondly, the terms *EVP* and *VOT*, which stand respectively for 'Electronic Voice Phenomenon' and 'Voices on Tape' and which have already been introduced:

Until the beginning of the 1980s, both terms were used to designate the recordings of anomalous voices on audio tapes that, thanks to the work of Friedrich Jürgenson and Dr. Konstantin Raudive, were attracting a great deal of attention throughout Europe. An alternative term also used in Great Britain and in the USA was 'Raudive Voices', thanks to the particular impact of Raudive's book published in English in 1971 under the title *Breakthrough*. For the most part I will use only the term EVP.

Researchers have received anomalous communications through EVP by a number of different methods, all of which I will describe in detail in the following chapters. The best-known of these methods uses an analogue or digital recorder together with a source of background noise, usually supplied by the so-called radio static or 'white noise'[1] produced when a radio is tuned between two stations. This 'white noise', which supplies a full spectrum of sound without any audible radio voices, provides an acoustic carrier from which the communicators supposedly modulate or construct their own voices (as yet there are no definitive conclusions as to the exact processes involved). Thus, this basic method can readily be used by any individual or group who has the interest and time to do so. No particular conditions, disposition, rituals or other esoteric practices are required. People who attempt contacts in this way are normally referred to as experimenters, researchers or operators, and these are the terms I shall use for them in this book.

The procedure involved in EVP is simple and offers no mystery. The experimenter turns on the recorder and the radio (or any other source of background noise later described in detail) and addresses a question (such as 'Can anyone hear me?') to the communicators he or she hopes may be present. The experimenter then remains silent for a minute or two while the tape or digital recorder continues to record the 'white noise'. Another question is then asked and the procedure is repeated. After working in this way for eight or ten minutes, the radio is turned off, the tape rewound (if a tape recorder is being used), and the recorded material is played back. The experimenter will hear the recorded 'white noise' and the questions, but will also hope to hear a, most likely, faint anomalous voice offering answers. Frequently nothing is heard, and it may take many weeks or months of patient and regular recording sessions before any results are obtained. If and when voices do occur they usually give two or three word answers to the experimenter's questions.

When the leading pioneer of ITC research, Friedrich Jürgenson, started his systematic work – following on from the puzzling and totally unexpected receipt of anomalous voices received while recording bird song for a documentary he was making – he reports that the 'voices' encouraged him to 'use the radio' (Jürgenson, 1964). At this point another extraordinary ITC phenomenon made its appearance, a phenomenon that has subsequently developed into a channel of communication that allows, in some cases, for much lengthier dialogues with communicators than is possible through EVP. Known as the *Direct Radio Voices (DRV)* method, this new channel allows the apparent communicators to interact with the experimenter on Earth by speaking directly through the loudspeaker of a radio. In consequence, anybody present in the room during the experimental session can listen to and even put questions to the communicators who sometimes even exchange views with those present. An astounding conversation can then take place.

I do not believe that there is anything in this world that can be so stunning and moving for the experimenter as these incredible voices that sometimes sound loud and clear in his or her own house and answer his/her questions. Common language does not seem sufficient to express the impact of these direct voices on the person who receives them. To hear a voice calling your name from the loudspeaker of the radio, as has happened to me several times during my own experiments, which then continues to say things such as – in my case – 'It is your grandmother' or 'It is João Cardoso speaking' (my deceased father's name) or 'It is Nisha' (one of my most beloved deceased dogs) – and then carry on a short conversation with you, arouses an emotion of such a powerful and amazing nature that I find no appropriate words to describe it. You feel you are in contact with the 'impossible' and how do you describe contact with the impossible?

Friedrich Jürgenson and Dr. Konstantin Raudive reported receiving these extraordinary voices in the 1960s (Jürgenson ibid, 1964; Raudive, 1968, 1971) and by the 1980s a surprising number of ITC contacts were being reported by researchers throughout Europe (Senkowski ibid, 1995). Contacts involving not only audio tape recorders, digital recorders and radios but virtually all the currently available electronic media devices followed, and an impressive array of evidence has built up. It was at this point that Professor Ernst Senkowski decided that the terms EVP or VOT, which at that time were still used to designate all electronic contacts by whatever methods, were no longer adequate, and the term ITC was proposed by him and generally accepted.

The third group of terms that require explanation are *Psychoimages or Transimages*. Klaus Schreiber, a modest German experimenter, who like almost all other researchers started by successfully using the EVP method, was apparently instructed by his deceased daughter Karine through an audio contact on how to start the methodology that would allow him to later receive anomalous visual images. After a wide range of experiments, Schreiber found that by filming the 'snow' caused by tuning a TV set to a blank channel and then projecting the result back onto the screen to be filmed again in a continuous feedback loop, anomalous images can sometimes be obtained. These images cannot be explained as stray television transmissions, and on a number of occasions have been shown to resemble known deceased people. The Psychoimages method is normally only used for a couple of minutes or less each time, because one minute of film can take up to an hour to view and scrutinize. The experimenter has to view the material frame by frame, but in doing so an anomalous image may become visible. In addition to people, animals and landscapes, supposedly of the next world, have been captured by this method, together with images of purportedly higher beings, such as those reportedly received by a group of experimenters based in Luxembourg and in Germany (more details later in the book). Throughout the book, I may occasionally use the term 'high entity', 'high power' or 'higher beings' and I would like to explain what I mean by those terms, commonly used in the esoteric literature and which I do not particularly like. I use them for simplification and economy of language and because they are easily understood. In my view, the so-called 'high entities' are presumably beings that encompass an expanded consciousness, the limits of which are not discernable by us. This would be the case of the Technician, of ABX Juno, and others. Such beings, normally of non-human, or any other physical origin, have called themselves 'no-names' and to me this seems more appropriate, although perhaps not so easily grasped.

Fourthly, although as yet no special terms are involved, ITC communications are also received through *computers and fax machines*. An impressive amount of anomalous information of high quality has been received through computers in particular. Such information appears either on the hard disk or the monitor and often the experimenters were informed by the communicators through DRV for instance of its impending transmission. The information is often of a high ethical nature and very detailed (Senkowski ibid, 1995; Locher and Harsch, 1989). The only procedure known to me that can be used in a deliberate attempt to obtain it is to leave the computer on night and day for an unspecified length of time with a special request addressed to the communicators showing on the monitor, and to wait for a reply. However, computer contacts are much rarer than voice communications.

Fifthly, we have *Anomalous Telephone Contacts* which we can refer to as *ATC*. Anomalous contacts through the telephone have been reported for almost a century. The Brazilian investigator, Oscar D'Argonnel, seems to have been the first to formally report these anomalous conversations (D'Argonnel, 1925). Since then, perhaps thousands of telephone contacts, apparently from the deceased, have been reported all over the world (Scott Rogo and Bayless, 1979; Brune, 2005; Senkowski ibid, 1995). This type of phenomena is, in fact, far more common than we would expect. Normally spontaneous, there is no method known to me by which we can invoke them.

As happens with all anomalous electronic phenomena – and in my view with all other types of communications from the deceased – it is the communicators who have the initiative and they are the ones who make the contacts happen (albeit with the contribution of the human partner on Earth). There seems to be no way that a human agent can summon these contacts – he or she can only be disposed and prepared to receive them. Certainly we can ask for them when trying the EVP, the DRV or the psychoimages methods, but the request will not necessarily be satisfied! It may be or it may not be.

The famous case of ABX Juno, the high entity that spoke with Peter Härting and Jochem Fornoff in Darmstadt, gives us valuable clues on this issue. ABX Juno once told Peter Härting and his colleagues: 'Again and again we are asked whether it is good to take up a connection to us from your side. See it in such a way: Without our friendly cooperation your most intensive efforts would be in vain' (Fornoff, 2009; Schäfer, 1993, p. 140).

As my communicators independently affirmed in reply to a question I had put to them, at the request of Professor David Fontana, on what the contacts depended upon, 'They depend on us.' This is, in my view, a point of extreme importance that I will discuss later.

Chapter 2

Brief Historical Survey

A substantial number of Western and Eastern traditions report on the use of instruments purportedly to establish contact with the so-called world of the spirits. According to some of these reports, either real or legendary, around 4,000 years ago the Chinese already consulted the spirits using rudimentary instruments (Spence, 1974). Dr. Hernani Guimarães Andrade, the renowned Brazilian psychical investigator who is mentioned in the previous chapter, describes one of these instruments, namely the Chi-Ti, which consisted basically of a forked pole whose movements when held by an operator were said to indicate responses from the spirits (e.g. Andrade ibid, 1997).

The well known Western device of the Ouija board, considered by some to facilitate communications with the deceased, is described by Fodor: 'As an invention [that] is very old. It was in use in the days of Pythagoras, about 540 B.C. According to a French historical account of the philosopher's life, his sect held frequent séances or circles at which "a mystic table, moving on wheels, moved towards signs, which the philosopher and his pupil, Philolaus, interpreted to the audience as being revelations supposedly from the unseen world"' (Fodor, 1974, p. 270). All such instruments, albeit in an elementary way, could be said to be predecessors of modern ITC practices that utilize electronic devices.

Jonathan Koons' Electromagnetic Battery

In modern times, the direct predecessor of ITC seems to be the electromagnetic battery of Jonathan Koons.

And I have to again mention my dear Brazilian friend's work, above cited, because it was by reading it that I got acquainted with this remarkable event which I had not previously seen quoted in the contemporary literature on psychical research, with the exception of a few earlier investigators of great knowledge, as is the case of the famous Italian researcher, Ernesto Bozzano. In the August, September and October 1925 issues of the *Révue Spirite*, Bozzano published a study on Koons' battery but unfortunately he did not possess the complete diagram of the apparatus; he only knew that it was composed of copper and zinc elements connected in a complex way. The great Spiritualist, Emma Hardinge Britten, refers to it in her classical, *Modern American Spiritualism* (1870), as does Dr. Robert Hare in *Experimental Investigations* (1855). Nandor Fodor (1974), in his *Encyclopaedia of Psychic Science*, reports on some of the events that apparently occurred in the wooden shed constructed by Koons according to the Spirits' instructions to be the place where contacts with another plane of existence would take place.

When Jonathan Koons joined Spiritualism in 1852, and apparently contacted the Spirits, he was informed that he and all his numerous children were powerful mediums. He constructed the electromagnetic battery rigorously, following the indications conveyed to him by the communicating entities. The battery seems to have been the first electrical instrument purposely designed and used to communicate with another level of existence.

Inside the wooden shed, there were several objects that could produce noise, mainly musical instruments. There were also two tables and material for direct writing. The mediums and the participants would sit at one of the tables and the electromagnetic battery was placed on top of the other table. The objects for the transcommunication with the spirits were placed around the battery. Accounts from that period inform us that the drums placed on the table would sound strongly and that the voices of the spirits could be heard from far away, speaking to the people present in the shed through a megaphone. Music pieces would be played on the instruments by the spirits, and human voice choirs singing very harmoniously were frequently heard.

There are other modern ITC situations where beautiful human choirs are addressed to us from the invisible dimension, as happens with Marcello Bacci (e.g. Bacci, 1985), and as has also happened with my own communications from Rio do Tempo Station, some of which consisted of wonderful musical pieces and choirs.

I have only referred to some of the most striking and successful cases of devices built under the communicators' guidance, starting with the instruction that tradition claims Jehovah imparted on Moses. But there are other cases thoroughly described by Dr. Hernani Guimarães Andrade in the excellent work I have cited.

When we analyze successful and unsuccessful cases of Instrumental Transcommunication contacts, it seems that we can draw an obvious conclusion – when the technical procedures are guided by the communicators themselves (e.g. Koons' battery, the Spiricom, the Harsch-Fischbach, etc. that we will study later), the communications flow easily and are highly successful. However, the same thing does not seem to happen when it is not the communicators but the experimenter who devises the means and the methods for the contact. For this reason, and also because it seems to imply that during such a remote epoch the communicators already thought of the possibility of using electricity as a privileged vehicle for their contacts, I find that Koons' electromagnetic battery is a very interesting example. Apparently, this was also the first successful experience of its kind.

The First Recordings

It was the American ethnographer, Waldemar Borogas, who in 1901 seems to have achieved the first registration of voices of unexplained origin, during an expedition to Siberia, while recording the invocations of the shamans Chukchees. The ethnographer himself reported on the occurrence in *The Chukchee Jesup North Pacific Expedition,* Vol. 7, II, p. 435 (Grandsire, 1998).

The phonograph was one of Thomas Alva Edison's many inventions, and he also invented the normal electric light bulb. The intention attributed to this genius among scientists of trying to build an apparatus to attempt the contact with the inhabitants of another dimension 'if they existed', as he put it, is a well known fact, especially with ITC researchers. Edison himself confirmed his interest to a journalist of the Belgian newspaper, *Le Soir* (Grandsire, 1998). When on the 26th of December 1920 the journalist questioned him on that issue, Edison replied:

I do not mean to say that our personality transits after death into another sphere for the simple reason that we do not know anything about that. But I hope to be able to build an apparatus of such high sensitivity that if the multitude of superior entities about whom I spoke with you survives they will have at their disposal this device to manifest their presence in a much safer way than the tables and the knocks on the walls! At the moment I can only make one comment about my apparatus i.e., that it will be able to multiply by an enormous number of times any infinitesimal effort one may conceive. It is comparable to the control board of a machine room where the effort of a human hand is sufficient to set a steam turbine of 50,000 horse power into movement. One of my closest collaborators died a few weeks ago. He knew the exact goal of my work. If his personality survives physical death he should be the first to manifest the survival of his ego. Drawings have been published that represent me communicating, through a kind of wireless radio, with the spirits of the dead. Nothing is more absurd. I repeat it once more; I do not aim at conversing with Cleopatra's or Napoleon's shadow... I aim solely at facilitating a tool to psychical research experts, one which will offer them the same service that the microscope rendered to biologists. Therefore, if the superior entities of the deceased, mainly of those who throughout their existence were familiar with the field of electricity, cannot influence my new apparatus I will have lost all hope in the survival of our personality.

Nevertheless, judging by the chronicles that reached us, Edison's machine would have yielded unimportant results or even no results at all. This is still an obscure point and one that has been the object of much speculation. However, Edison undoubtedly favored the survival concept and wrote in *The People*, October 29, 1926:

My researches tend strongly to support the view of life after death, and I am even inclined to support the view that communication is possible.

Another great figure of science, Guglielmo Marconi, also considered the possibility of contacting the next world through Hertzian waves – his intentions were privately confirmed by his wife after his death, although we do not possess details of any possible attempts he may have made. The same is said about one of the most important inventors in history, Nikola Tesla, but again in his case we have no proper evidence to confirm the stories that are frequently disseminated in radio and television programs about ITC.

Communications Through Human Mediumship Announce the Advent of ITC

Although Instrumental Transcommunication has reached its status as an effective method for research into the hypothesis of the survival of physical death, and apparently for the communication with the deceased (largely through the work and creative inspiration of its great pioneer Friedrich Jürgenson, and through the meticulous systematic work of Dr. Konstantin Raudive, who followed on his footsteps), this 'new way' started to be announced to mankind long before the middle of the 20th century, when it became visible. As early as the middle of the 19th century, we already received a hint through mediumistic communications reported by Allan Kardec, in *The First Book of the Spirits*, that the means of communication would radically change in future contacts. I'll quote Question 468:

Is not the loss of those who are dear to us a legitimate source of sorrow, seeing that this loss is both irreparable and independent of our action?

Reply:

This cause of sorrow, which acts alike upon rich and poor, is the common law of humanity, for it is either a trial or an expiation; but you have the consolation of holding communication with your friends through the means already possessed by you, that develop further every day, **while awaiting other means that will be more direct, and more accessible to your senses**.

In the *Revue Spirite*, of which Kardec was the editor, I found the following passage in one of the articles on information received through human mediumship:

...reflecting on the difficulty that we experience when we contact the mediums and use their faculties, you will be kind enough to pass over certain expressions or certain forms of language that we cannot always control. **Later on, electricity will make its mediumistic revolution, and since everything**

will then be changed in the way of reproducing the thought of the Spirit you will no longer find such defaults, which are sometimes regrettable especially when the communications are read in front of strangers. (Kardec, 1864)

Later, in 1936, publisher Paul Leymarie published Suzanne Max Getting's *Messages by a Liberated Spirit* (Grandsire, 1998). The 26th of these messages, dated 2nd February 1930, states that:

...the Spiritualist movement is beginning to spread. The role of mediums in the future...We will speak to you through the medium of the phonograph and you will see us on film... the medium will play a passive role in the future.

... In many cases the devices will replace the work of the mediums ... We will thus do without the mediums through the phonograph. The medium will only be present as a source of energy, producing a benign atmosphere through his vibrations... We will be able to impress the rolls of the phonograph through the vibrations of our waves. In this form our thoughts will be captured as are the sound waves of human voices that you nowadays record. Once recorded, our vibrations will be totally identical to those produced by the human voice... It is a work of adaptation...The waves emanating from the entities do not possess the same tones as those produced by a human voice box. A very refined product that will be impressed with extreme ease will therefore be necessary. It will allow us to dictate to a phonograph as we dictate to a medium... This invention is not yet ready, naturally, but it is already under study in some supra-terrestrial worlds...

Similar information on the future electronic communication has been received through other reputable mediums in other parts of the world (Meek, 1987).

Modern ITC Contacts

Parapsychologists David Scott Rogo and Raymond Bayless extensively describe another ITC phenomenon – the *Phone Calls from the Dead* – in their book with the same title (1979). Since we are concerned here mainly with the verbal taped communications, I will not get into details of the impressive amount of phone calls described by Scott Rogo and Bayless in their work. Indeed, they seem to be a fairly common occurrence. The last chapter of the book is dedicated to the *Electronic Contact with the Dead: a Wider Perspective* (p. 117). The authors managed to assemble, in this section, an excellent historical résumé of the first attempts at electronic communication with the deceased. Unfortunately, the range of their work is limited to the English language, the one they had access to, and therefore it lacks the important information published in other European languages besides English.

They start with David Wilson, a London solicitor and an amateur wireless operator. Wilson already reported some of his experiments that seemed to yield coherent messages to the March 13, 1915 issue of *Light*. These were transmitted through the Morse alphabet and he continued publishing some of his results in *Light*, some of which involved the presence of reliable witnesses; Scott Rogo and Bayless affirm that there were many similar instances published by radio operators, who believed that they had received communications from the Beyond during the early years of telegraphy. They also mention an English inventor, F. R. Melton, who, in 1921, claimed he had invented a 'psychic telephone'. In a booklet published that same year, under the title *A Psychic Telephone*, Melton gives details and diagrams of the device.

But one of the most concerted efforts to achieve purely instrumental contact with the dead was carried out in Holland by Dr. J. L. Matla and Dr. G. J. Zaalbert, both trained physicists who initiated their research in 1904. According to Rogo and Bayless, in their book, *Le Mystère de la Mort* (The Mystery of Death), they report their successful and consistent results to contact the dead through their ingenious and complex devices that they called the 'manometer' and a later one, the 'dynamistograph'. They report that this machine, like the manometer, was often left in the empty experimental room, and yet it would type out meaningful communications even when the scientists were totally absent from the building. One of Dr. Matla's most interesting conclusions is that 'the very element of our personality that survives death is partially electrical in nature and has an affinity for manipulating electrical energy' (Scott Rogo and Bayless, ibid). If we compare this affirmation with Rio do Tempo's information that 'our [their] bodies are made of a kind of electricity' we wonder about the remarkable coincidence.

I myself had an extraordinary experience in this field. When one of my Doberman puppies, Michi, was dying, I stayed by her throughout the whole process keeping my hand on her chest/tummy. Almost simultaneously with her expiring I felt a kind of tickling electrical vibration coming through my hand as if something had crossed it for a moment and then disappeared. This was the only time in my life I felt this sensation that had never happened before in any kind of electrical occurrences, and which I, therefore, cannot compare with anything else. It was similar to an electrical shock but finer, lighter and much more pleasant. Rainer Holbe, the journalist who closely followed the work of several ITC German researchers, quotes some of Karin's many EVP messages to her father, Klaus Schreiber, on page 32 of his book on Schreiber's experiments (Italian translation). Said she: 'We are an incarnation of the electricity' a very interesting affirmation that is relevant to our discussion (Holbe, 1989).

It appears that the accidental discovery of the extraordinary voices on tape fell to two Catholic priests and scientists, Father Agostino Gemelli, the founder of the Catholic University of Milan and President of the Pontifical Academy, and Father Pellegrino Ernetti, a Benedictine monk at the famous Abbey of

San Giorgio Maggiore in Venice. Indeed they seem to have been the first people to record identifiable paranormal voices. On September 17, 1952, the priests were working on the recording of Gregorian chants at the Laboratory of Physics at the Catholic University of Milan, with the recorders of that time that used wire instead of magnetic tape. The work was constantly interrupted by the rupture of the wire. On one of those occasions, Father Gemelli, in exasperation, called out to his deceased father for help, a habit of his when he was in difficulties. After repairing the wire and upon listening to the recording the priests suddenly heard, instead of the Gregorian chant, the voice of Gemelli's father saying 'Of course I help you, I am always with you'. The priests were utterly amazed and Father Gemelli repeated the experiment by asking 'Is it really you, Papa?', and to their great surprise the recorded reply came 'Of course it is me. Don't you recognize me 'Testone' [the nickname the father used to call him when he was a child]?'

Extremely impressed, the priests requested an interview with Pope Pious XII, to whom they told the whole story. The Pope seemed very pleased, and put the worried priests at ease by telling them that 'Tape recorders cannot be influenced.' He then declared that these results could mark 'the beginning of a new scientific study that would confirm faith in the Beyond and in the teachings of the Church about life after death,' (Brune, 1988).

In the book I mentioned before, Scott Rogo also reports on the first experiments with the tape voice phenomenon developed by Attila von Szalay in 1956. Von Szalay was immediately joined by Raymond Bayless and their experimentation lasted into the mid 1970s. Great success was obtained and Bayless' first announcement of this discovery and early tests was published in the *Journal of the American Society of Psychical Research*, January, 1959, but the parapsychological community at large ignored the astounding breakthrough.

The voices they recorded had all the characteristics of the

voices which later on became known as EVP. One of the interesting coincidences is the fact that he mentions that some of the
voices recorded with von Szalay 'yelled' and that sometimes they
also produced a lot of whistles (e.g. Scott Rogo and Bayless ibid,
pp. 89 and 85 respectively). As I will report later in the book,
some of my own earlier voices very markedly yelled and I also
have recordings where they seem to reply to me with whistles.
Scott Rogo also reports that these phenomena were produced
whether '...von Szalay was in or out of the cabinet...' And he
adds, 'Only a few words were spoken at a time, and the voices
were both male and female in quality. Often, they sounded rather
mechanical.'

In my opinion, it is highly significant to find that, as early as
the very beginning of the electronic voices, there is already a
striking parallel between the characteristics of some of those very
first voices and voices recorded many years later. This is the case
of some of my own and some of the voices received in
Luxembourg, amongst others, which can also sound rather
mechanical.

However, it was not until 1959 when Friedrich Jürgenson, the
well known Swedish painter, musician and cinema director,
recorded anomalous voices that real, consistent research into
what was later called EVP began. He is undoubtedly the great
pioneer of ITC. His interest for the subject was aroused when,
while recording the song of night birds in his beautiful property
'Nysund' (Sweden) for the sound track of a documentary film on
the life of birds, he accidentally recorded his first EVP voice. The
experience was repeated a number of times, with voices that
spoke to him in German, Italian, Hungarian, and Swedish
(Jürgenson, like many other famous ITC researchers, was multi-
lingual and was fluent in some eight languages). The voices gave
him several identification names (among them those of members
of his own family) and called him by his pet name, thus
convincing Jürgenson that he was indeed listening to the dead

(Jürgenson ibid, 1964).

Subsequently, he presented his findings to the Swedish Society of Parapsychological Research, but as had happened with Raymond Bayless in the USA, he found little interest among parapsychologists. Undeterred, he continued his experiments and even abandoned his professional and artistic life to dedicate himself full-time to the voice research. He spent long solitary periods in his country house away from his own family and friends, relentlessly working with the voices, listening to his recordings over and over until he had properly identified each word of the communications.

In 1964 he published *Voices from the Space* and later *Radio Communications with the Dead*. The late Professor Hans Bender, who is considered by many to be the most eminent European parapsychologist of the 20th century, and Director of the Institute of Parapsychology at the University of Freiburg, became interested and investigated Jürgenson's work thoroughly. In the company of technicians, technical advisers and physicists from the University and elsewhere, Bender carried out meticulous experiments with Jürgenson in 1964 and again in 1970 in Germany and Sweden. As a precaution, he used a number of different tape recorders and precise unidirectional microphones with radio filters that eliminated the possibility of picking up random sounds. Even the electrical cables were kept very short to avoid the remote chance of capturing stray radio signals. Various different oscilloscopes were used, as well as television cameras, and electromagnetic wave detectors were set up to analyze the environment of the different laboratories in which the experiments took place, so that the equipment could be set up in areas where the levels were at their lowest. Using these strict controls, some of the most important recordings were made in the presence of Dr. Keil, Director of the Department of Psychology at Tasmania University, and an army of technicians (Bender, 1970, 1976).

Hans Bender was adamant that the results of the experiments could not be explained by normal means. However, he himself remained skeptical about the possibility of survival, and preferred to attribute the phenomena to psychokinesis by Jürgenson.

Friedrich Jürgenson was a renowned personality in the European cultural milieu of the middle of the 20th century and, therefore, his discovery had a wide projection. Renowned scientists and European public figures received the information through his many conferences, articles, radio and television programs; and when this astonishing phenomenon was made public for the first time it initiated a great movement of curiosity and interest, especially in Europe.

One of the personalities that became interested and intrigued by it was Konstantin Raudive, a Latvian philosopher and literary scholar educated at the Sorbonne and at the University of Salamanca, with Swedish nationality, who would later be the first person to systematize the study of EVP. With great interest in philosophy and parapsychology and with published work to his credit, Dr. Raudive worked with Jürgenson for a few years but from 1969 onwards the two men worked separately. Raudive captured over 70,000 EVP voices with a simple tape recorder. In addition to his work with the voice phenomena, Raudive became well known as a consequence of his scholarly background and his reputation in psychical research. In 1968 he published *Unhörbares Wird Hörbar – Auf den Spuren Einer Geisterwelt* and this was followed, a few years later, by the English translation, *Breakthrough: An Amazing Experiment in Electronic Communication with the Dead* (see e.g. Raudive, 1971).

Before bringing out this translation, the English publisher, Colin Smythe, arranged for Raudive's work to be put to scientific test. With the technical assistance of electro-acoustics experts, Ray Prickett and Ken Attwood, and in the presence of Colin Smythe, Peter Bander, Sir Robert Mayer and Raudive himself, and under the supervision of the aforementioned experts (from Pye Records), four tape recorders (the principal recorder being made by Nagra, a Swiss company, and it was quite well shielded from radio interference[1]) were set to record for 18 minutes. Instruments revealed that recordings were taking place although the listeners could hear nothing through their headphones. On rewinding and playing the tapes over 200 voices, of which 27 were clearly understandable, were heard. Speaking with Philip Newell, whom I know well, Ray Prickett, one of the two experts from Pye Records, claimed not to have heard a single, intelligible word during those tests.[2] Interestingly, on page 60 of his *Carry on Talking, How Dead Are the Voices?* Peter Bander says about the two technicians:

> At revolution 250, the control device suddenly registered a strong series of signals. Ken Attwood was very excited, assuring us that this just could not happen. Prickett, on the other hand, still checking the oscillator,[3] called out that not a single signal was being registered at his end... Of course the observations by the two engineers contradict each other. How was it possible that one device registered signals and the other did not?

And he further clarifies that the two devices were synchronized and in perfect balance. This is, of course, a very out of the ordinary event – the control device under Attwood's supervision registered signals, while the one handled by Prickett did not. Could it be explained by the unconscious effect of Prickett's mind, who is recognizably antagonistic to the voice phenomenon, on the sensitive electronic devices? It is an interesting question that must remain open, at least until we understand the functioning of the psyche better than we do today.

Sir Robert Mayer recognized one of the voices recorded on this occasion as that of Arthur Schanabel, a friend who had recently died (Bander ibid, 1972). It was also considered that a voice was heard which was said to be that of the recently deceased orchestral conductor, Sir John Barbirolli, who was well known to Sir Robert, but it is also interesting to note that the late Ken Attwood had also been involved in the recordings of Barbirolli just before his death.[4]

I could continue sharing with my readers the episodes of the highly interesting saga Dr. Raudive lived while in England, but the readers particularly interested in knowing the details of this story will find an excellent source in Peter Bander's book, *Carry on Talking, How Dead Are the Voices?*, already quoted above.

A second series of experiments was held in a technical laboratory of Belling and Lee, in Enfield, England. This laboratory was equipped with a shield for radio frequencies which prevented the intrusion of the electro-magnetic waves. Peter Hale, an expert in electrical screening techniques, and Ralph Lovelock, a physicist and electronics expert, supervised the recordings, during which a series of clear EVP voices was again captured.

Undeterred by skeptics who tried all means to undermine his work, Raudive continued his labor, developing the theory of an 'opposed world', an alternative level of reality intimately connected to our own, where the spirits of the dead live and try to communicate with us. A large number of Raudive's recordings have been preserved in Münster, Westfalia, in Germany, and another collection has recently come into the possession of the British Society for Psychical Research and been given by them to the British National Acoustics Laboratory.

I can never overemphasize the fact that Friedrich Jürgenson's and Konstantin Raudive's books are basic pillars in the already extensive literature on this subject, and that their reading ought to be compulsory for any keen ITC experimenter or theoretical researcher.

In the USA, George Meek, a man of great vision and

intelligence, had an amazing attitude, and performed one of these gestures that seem to belong more to legend than to the real petty life we are unfortunately so used to. He retired at sixty in order to be able to devote his still dynamic energy, creativity and millionaire fortune to the incredible enterprise of 'establishing a communication system capable of allowing two-way conversation with the higher levels of consciousness without the intervention of the human mind' (e.g. Meek, 1987). And his intrepid, visionary spirit led him to be responsible for groundbreaking experiments. Engineer, inventor and prosperous businessman when he retired in 1960, he established the Metascience Foundation in Franklin, North Carolina, USA, in order to carry out research into all the possibilities capable of making his supreme goal come true. Hearing of ITC during one of his trips to Europe, Meek used leading mediums in an attempt to contact deceased scientists and technicians with a view to obtaining information on how to improve ITC contacts.

One of these psychics, William O'Neil, who was also an electronics engineer, received instruction for the construction of a highly complex device that combined the emission and reception of electromagnetic waves with certain acoustic elements. Thus, the famous 'Spiricom' was born, and through it O'Neil was apparently able to contact Dr. George Mueller, a scientist, who had died in 1967 (Meek ibid, 1987). Details of Mueller's life, unknown to the researchers, were given mostly through clairaudient messages received by O'Neil and carefully put down on tape by the latter, and later found to be correct. Mueller was a frequent communicator through the Spiricom constructed by O'Neil under Mueller's technical guidance. In 1982, Meek demonstrated the Spiricom to a press conference at the National Press Club in Washington D.C. Sadly, however, the success of Spiricom was short-lived. Dr. Mueller warned that the contact could not long be maintained, and his words turned out to be correct. However, enough had been discovered to prompt Meek to spend the rest of his life presenting the Spiricom and other ITC results worldwide, with the aim of demonstrating that objective contact can be established with another level of reality without the intervention of the human mind through mediumship, and to the satisfaction of many scientists (see also Fuller, 1985).

In the USA, the pioneering role of experimentation with the voices on tape belonged to a small and fragile lady full of determination and courage, Sarah Estep, who in 1976 learned about the phenomenon through a description of Friedrich Jürgenson's and Konstantin Raudive's work and decided to start her own experimentation. In her book, *Voices of Eternity*, published in 1988, which is also an excellent manual on the voice phenomenon, Sarah describes step by step the interesting story of her skepticism and reluctant attempts to establish contact with another dimension, in her view an incredible possibility, which nevertheless yielded positive results and made of her one of the most enthusiastic precursors of the systematic work with EVP. She founded the American Association of Electronic Voice Phenomena in 1982, and a few years before her recent death in 2008 published another book, *Roads to Eternity* (Estep, 2005). The AA-EVP is presently directed by Tom and Lisa Butler, who spare no efforts, and have managed to develop the Association in a creative and innovative way.

In South America the phenomenon extended to many countries where associations flourish and many thousands of people experiment. One of the most prolific of these is Brazil where, due to the national well known interest in the so-called esoteric matters and under the patronage of Dr. Hernani Guimarães Andrade, knowledge and information about ITC events were received with great joy and enthusiasm, and led to the constitution of the ANT (Associação Nacional de Transcomunicadores) directed by Sonia Rinaldi, an organization that currently numbers thousands of experimenters and enthusiasts.

One of the figures who, because of their technical and/or

scientific background started by dismissing the phenomenon as 'impossible' but later became their ardent adepts, is electronics engineer Hans Otto König. Originally a skeptic, König set out to demonstrate the impossibility of ITC contacts. However, in the course of his work he found himself receiving voices of great clarity, some of which appeared to be from his deceased mother and deceased friends. Convinced of the reality of the voices, König then developed a series of complex devices, such as his now famous 'fields generator', which generates rectangular electromagnetic waves in the band of ultrasound that are then mixed, modulated, demodulated and filtered through a complex electronic system. König has become famous in the history of ITC both for the development of the fields' generator and for one of the most remarkable ITC experiments ever carried out in public. Invited by Radio Luxembourg to demonstrate direct radio dialogue with the next world live on television and radio, König apparently succeeded in doing so for two million listeners and viewers under the supervision of Radio Luxembourg's technicians and sound engineers. One of those present was George Meek, to whom the voices referred by name. Rainer Holbe, the prestigious television announcer who presented König's dialogue with the next world, and who confirmed on air that there was no possible way in which the voices could have been faked, subsequently followed up König's work, publicly defending the latter's sometimes defamed integrity, and publishing work of his own that adds significantly to ITC literature.

Rainer Holbe also followed up the work of another remarkable ITC researcher, Klaus Schreiber, the great pioneer of anomalous images on video tape and other media (Holbe, 1987); this work reached its most impressive level with the research of Maggy and Jules Harsch-Fischbach of Luxembourg. The images and the computer texts, some of them received in public by the Harsch-Fischbachs over a number of years, represent some of the most important data ever collected in the history of survival-of-death research. The images remain unparalleled in their objectivity, clarity and quality, as do the contents of the extraordinary verbal DRV messages and computer texts also received in the course of their work. As normally happens in ITC research, the Harsch-Fischbachs began by trying for EVP messages, receiving in the process instructions from their communicators on how to build and set up complex arrangements of equipment, some of which was also built to the recommendations of an entity said never to have been incarnated, who agreed to be called the Librarian, Archivist or Technician of planet Earth (see e.g. Locher and Harsch, 1995).

The contacts received by the Harsch-Fischbachs were by all known forms of ITC, including the telephone; and in their own home on July 1, 1988, for the first time in history, and following the instructions recommended by the Technician, sound and image of another level of reality were heard and seen simultaneously, orchestrated, it was said, by the then-deceased Konstantin Raudive. The setting for the extraordinary events, which happened with the Harsch-Fischbach couple, was investigated by technicians and scientists from all over the world, who themselves were present when direct dialogues with the next world were held, and images and voices of unmatched quality and clarity were received. Among these technicians and scientists were Father Andreas Resch, Prof. Dr. Dr., Founder and Head of the Institute of Border Sciences in Innsbruck/Austria, former visiting Professor at the Lateran University in Rome; George Meek; Dr. Ernst Senkowski; Dr. Ralph Determeyer; Father François Brune (Brune 2005, 2006).

In Germany, Homes and Malkhoff were also obtaining their results using equipment built to the instructions of the Technician and, as had happened in Luxembourg, receiving communications from entities identifying themselves as Wernher von Braun, Einstein, Raudive, Jürgenson, Klaus Schreiber, Manfred Boden, Seth 3 (who claimed to be from the 'fifth plane') and other famous personalities from Earth (Senkowski, 1999). In a recent exchange of correspondence with me about Adolf Homes, Ernst Senkowski wrote about this outstanding experimenter:

It is my conviction that the Homes' phenomena in their entirety have been the most comprising worldwide. They present the full ITC spectrum and as Dr. Delavre and I followed the case closely we are absolute sure of Homes' sincerity and reliability. In many cases he was completely overrun by what happened. He had no technical-electronic background at all, and in a certain way was a 'drop-out' barely apt to support his family...

Communications in Germany and Luxembourg also came from family members in the next world (Adolf Homes' deceased mother seemed to be for him the connecting link), as did images of animals, some of them deceased pets of the experimenters, as well as landscapes said by the communicators to be from their world. The voices claimed to speak through a special arrangement (supposedly of devices and other unknown elements) which they called 'Bridges' as we will discuss in a later chapter. From a technical point of view, it is important to stress that, as with the Spiricom, none of the pieces of equipment constructed in Luxembourg and elsewhere, to the specifications of the spirit communicators, make any sense in normal electro-acoustic terms.

So-called 'cross correspondences' (complementary or identical messages received through investigators working in isolation from each other) also occurred between the researchers in Luxembourg and Adolf Homes and Friedrich Malkhoff who lived near the German town of Trier. These included communications that were started by the communicating entities in Germany and finished by them in Luxembourg, and vice versa. The announcement would be made in Germany of the time and place at which a contact would be made in Luxembourg, and the same messages or images appeared spontaneously and simultaneously on the computer screens of both the Harsch-Fischbachs in Luxembourg and of Homes and Malkhoff in Germany. The entities involved in this work identified themselves as belonging to 'Zeitstrom' (i.e. 'Timestream' in English or 'Rio do Tempo' in Portuguese) Station and claimed to be supervised by the Technician, to be technically guided by Dr. Swejen Salter, and to be philosophically led by Dr. Konstantin Raudive. While communicating with Luxembourg in the 1980s, Raudive introduced Carlos de Almeida (said to belong to the Portuguese Group within Timestream), who then spoke directly to Luxembourg in Portuguese and gave the Group's Portuguese name 'Rio do Tempo'.

In Germany another famous case happened. The late Peter Härting, his wife and Jochem Fornoff started experimenting with a small group of friends by the middle of the eighties. Peter Härting was a sound engineer at the theater in Darmstadt and, as a consequence of his specialization in the field of acoustics, had strong doubts about the possibility of communication with another dimension through electronic devices. But Peter and Gisela Härting were also open-minded people, and in April 1987 they received astonishing communications through Direct Radio Voices from a non-human high entity that called itself ABX Juno. At the request of the experimenters, the high entity explained that A meant 'aussen' or 'ausserhalb' (from outside our terrestrial limitation), B meant biological and X meant experiment, while Juno was its name. Messages of important ethical and philosophical content were received by the group for some time through the 'Euro Bridge of Contact'. One of those said: 'Technique (or technology) does not replace the power of thought' (see Fornoff, 2009 for a complete survey of ABX Juno communications).

A German lady, Hildegard Schäfer, played an important role

in ITC research. Author of a first book on her personal experiences after losing her 23-year-old daughter, she wrote another book a few years later, which I strongly recommend to anybody interested in the subject or in starting personal experimentation. *Brücke Zwischen Diesseits und Jenseits* is the best manual for the beginner I can think of. In it she makes a remarkable compilation of the methods used by different experimenters and of the history of the subject until the late 1980s, when the work was published.

Hanna Buschbeck was another German personality who had a dynamic influence in this area. A pioneer, she started experimenting in 1968 after reading Jürgenson's book, *Radio Contacts with the Dead*. After meeting him personally, she decided to dedicate the rest of her life to ITC work, playing an important role in bringing together national and international researchers that, at the time, were still rare and unconnected. The most prominent figures of the field, from Jürgenson to Professor Hans Bender, Professor Alex Schneider, Germán de Argumosa, Professor Walter Uphoff and many others, met annually at her residence for enriching international debates in which the interchange of opinions and experiences played a vital role.

It would have been unforgivable not to mention in this chapter the work developed by the German physicist, Dr. Ernst Senkowski, to whom I have referred previously, towards the spreading and understanding of ITC phenomena. Himself a successful ITC experimenter, Professor Senkowski closely followed the experiments and results of several ITC researchers, namely Adolf Homes, the Luxembourg couple Jules and Maggy Harsch-Fischbach and others all over the world. Through such an extensive survey and the discussions carried out with the communicating entities in Luxembourg and at Adolf Homes' house, as well as through his own knowledge of physics, his intelligence, and his finely-tuned perception of life, he gained a comprehension of the phenomenon which is presently unequalled.

In Italy, the electro-magnetic voices have been investigated and studied by personalities of high technical profile, as is the case of Dr. Eng. Carlo Trajna, who even developed a theory to explain the production of the voices. Dr. Trajna developed the *Psychotemporal Model* theory, which is based upon the idea that psychic (or subjective) time flows at a different rhythm to physical time (the time measured by clocks). He also considers that the 'psycho-temporal wave' produced by four operators (an ideal number for the experimentation according to Trajna) will allow for the reception of longer ITC messages. The four operators figure, indicated by Trajna, does not necessarily imply four live experimenters; that number may consist of one live experimenter (or more) while the remaining may be discarnate entities.

The translation into English of his work has been published in issues number 1 to 7 of the ITC Journal (2000-2001). Also, according to Trajna, the voices speak mostly in the range of certain frequencies that he has enumerated. However, I have to confess that my personal experience does not confirm Trajna's theory about the frequencies because in my case the communicators have stated that 'to modulate the waves we [they] only need the short waves' (in the scope of the DRV), and also that the frequency in itself is not important; it is rather the type of noise produced by the radio and used as a carrier that may or may not be suitable for their work.

Italy has generated a number of remarkable ITC experimenters and investigators. One of these was Gabriella Alvisi, who experimented in ITC for many years and received striking voice contacts. I have been fortunate to have had access to a copy of one of her tapes published with one of her books, and could personally verify the quality and interesting content of some of her messages (Alvisi, 1983). I warmly thank Paolo Presi for kindly sending me a copy of his Alvisi tape and for buying her book for me. Another excellent Italian experimenter was Rafaella

Gremese who, in the early 1980s, experimented successfully with voices and mainly with transimages (Locher and Harsch, 1995, ibid p. 172). But the most outstanding Italian researcher is undoubtedly the untiring Marcello Bacci, whom I mentioned above, who at the Psychophonic Center of Grosseto has been experimenting with anomalous voice communications for over 40 years. For many years a small group, comprised primarily of the now deceased Luciano Capitani, Sergio Giomi, Sylvana Pagnotta and Bacci himself, met at the Psychophonic Center in Grosseto, and after years of assiduous and indefatigable endeavors, started obtaining extraordinary results consisting of two-way conversations through a radio set with entities who mostly identified themselves as the deceased, and who would often finish their contacts with a beautiful choir of heavenly voices. At the center in Grosseto, bereaved parents have assembled weekly with Bacci and his friends in the hope of hearing a word from a deceased child, parent or friend, and many of them affirm that they have indeed maintained conversations with their deceased loved ones. The Bacci contacts will usually last around 30 minutes. I have been privileged to have participated more than once at the extraordinary evenings which happen regularly at Grosseto. I had also the privilege of conversing with the entities, and on one of those occasions I carried on a conversation with the communicators in Portuguese only, and received a number of replies from them in my mother tongue. I believe that Marcello Bacci can rightly be considered the modern-day reference for DRV communications.

A large number of other successful ITC experimenters have grown in Italy, a country that has notably contributed to the advance of psychical research. One important Italian initiative was the creation in Bologna, some years ago, of *Il Laboratorio*, an institution dedicated to the scientific study and investigation of the so-called paranormal phenomena. Directed by the well known parapsychologist, Dr. Enrico Marabini, it integrates a team of technicians who endeavor to apply sophisticated technical methods to the examination of different kinds of anomalous phenomena with particular emphasis on ITC communications, e.g. images and voices.

In France, Monique Simonet was a pioneer of the anomalous voices research. Like many other ITC researchers all over the world, this lovely and brave lady started experimenting at the beginning of the 1970s, after listening to a radio program on Jürgenson's and Raudive's voices. She obtained good results and since then dedicated her life to helping the bereaved by generously trying to establish contacts with their deceased loved ones. Author of a number of books on the anomalous voices and the anomalous images that she also pursued, Monique was the founder of the French EVP Association Infinitude. Showing great competence and dedication, Jacques and Monique Blanc-Garin have continued her work at Infinitude, an organization devoted chiefly to helping people who suffered the loss of a loved one, as well as to ITC experimentation and research in general. Presently, Infinitude has over 1,700 associates, many of whom are also successful EVP experimenters.

When we speak of ITC and France there is an important international figure that deserves particular mention. Theologian Father Dr. François Brune has been the herald of the 'new way' of communication throughout the world. One of his books, *Les Morts Nous Parlent*, is a bestseller translated into dozens of languages. 'Père Brune', as he is affectionately known in many countries, has witnessed many of the most significant contacts anywhere in the world. A catholic priest, Father Brune has spared no effort to spread the 'good news', as he calls ITC, through his frequent international conferences, public presentations and participation wherever information about survival of physical death is necessary.

In Spain, parapsychologists Germán de Argumosa and Sinesio Darnell are pioneers of high standard. They started their own research at the beginning of the seventies, after hearing of

Jürgenson's voices, and since then they have indefatigably dedicated a lot of their time and energy to research, particularly in the field of psychophony, as the phenomenon is known in Spain.

I have only mentioned some of the main experimenters and researchers in the area of Instrumental Transcommunication but there are actually thousands of people in the world who experiment in ITC and obtain results, many of which may be significant, although we have no information about them. Maybe the time predicted by the communicators, when the contact with their world will become part of daily life, is not far off. However, we should also keep in mind that our restricted measure of time as individuals has not much meaning, not only in terms of human evolution, but also from the point of view of the communicators who, in their own words, 'live outside of time' (Cardoso 2003, 2005). Hence, who knows what will happen, and when?

Chapter 3

First Experiences

The Beginning

It all started in Galicia, the beautiful, mysterious north-westernmost region of Spain, where my career had brought me as Consul General of Portugal in 1994. It was such a homely destination; a place so close to Portugal that it almost seemed inappropriate to call it a diplomatic post. Days went by, pleasant and unpretentious, without much to speak about in comparison with some of my former destinations; for instance, fantastic India where I went through terrible and dangerous times in the aftermath of Indira Gandhi's murder; or Japan, with its exotic, complicated mentality that can create all kinds of difficulties and conflicts when it interacts with the Western way of life.

A diplomatic post abroad is always a tiring but exciting adventure, at least at the beginning, and the simplicity of my new destination seemed boring to some. I remember how my brother Luis became puzzled and saddened when I told him I was coming to Galicia, and said he regretted that I had chosen a destination that was not compatible with the professional level I had already attained in my career. But I found it welcoming, cozy, and peaceful. It was like a haven after almost twenty years of wandering throughout the world in far away and quite difficult places. It was quiet, healthy, beautiful and uncomplicated. I needed it too – my long, traumatic, emotionally devastating relationship had very recently culminated in divorce, and the grief caused by the recent deaths of several treasured family members and friends was still very poignant and painful.

I started to heal by looking every morning at the beautiful Atlantic Ocean from the window of my bedroom, swimming in its tranquil waters whenever I could and strolling in the solitary hill paths of a rugged land all made of granite, home of Romans, Celts, Visigoths, and present-day Galicians – simple, honest and hard working people. Slowly I became more tranquil, a feeling I had not experienced for many years.

Throughout my life I have always liked to share with those around me my interests, my likings, my joys and pains. Although I greatly appreciate solitude, I am an extrovert and above all I am not a secretive person. I soon became friends with the staff at the Consulate-General and used to exchange views with them frequently on the topics of my concern – among them a keen interest in the research of the possibility of survival of physical death. This circumstance brought to my knowledge interesting experiences that some of them had gone through following the deaths of their loved ones.

One day in the summer of 1997, one of the officers at the Consulate-General, a man of literary and intellectual concerns, came to me with a very special request. A lady friend of his had asked him fervently to arrange an interview with me. He told me the lady was in a terrible psychological and physical state and that they feared for her life. She had, in effect, already attempted to commit suicide three times and if she had not managed to do it, it was only because of her husband's constant vigilance of her. This was the result of the sudden death of her 18-year-old only son in a sailing accident in the Bay of Vigo in mysterious and foul circumstances. The parents suspected that the tragedy involved the negligence of the people in charge of a ship of a powerful multinational company that was crossing the bay at the same time of the boy's supposed accident.

She had heard that I had some knowledge in the field of survival research and felt that I was her only hope. Very reluctantly I agreed to receive her in my house but I did not believe I could do much for her because my own knowledge of the subject, although greater than most people, was quite modest and principally because I myself had no certainty of any kind about survival of physical death and had instead all kinds of doubts.

This woman, who later became my friend and of whom I reserve the full name to respect her privacy, came into my garden one beautiful summer afternoon and she was like the figure of a Greek tragedy all dressed in white, her pale face covered by her long blond hair, and big sunglasses that could not hide the swelling of her poor eyes. She walked slowly, dragging her slight 39 kilograms with great difficulty. I felt my heart shrink and a great empathy started to grow between us. From then on we met several times in my house where she always came with her husband, who cared for her constantly.

They were then an intellectual couple, forty years old, modern, politically aware, highly concerned with environmental issues, living in a comfortable economic situation; people who were not prepared for the sudden, unexpected death of their only son, a beautiful boy of eighteen. Athletic, intelligent, well-behaved little Juan was their pride and joy. The three of them had formed a bond of love and sharing that they thought was indestructible. It was obvious that they had not yet accepted that their lives could have been shattered in such a brutal way when their boy was sailing happily in the calm waters of the 'Ría' of Vigo on a beautiful summer's day.

I shared with them what I knew about the evidence provided by the research into survival of physical death – the existence of some impressive messages of mediumistic origin that are part of the classical literature on the subject, and some information on the development of a new form of communication known as Instrumental Transcommunication that seemed to have yielded amazing results. Because of my linguistic education I could buy and read different works written in several European languages and thus my sources were varied and the most reliable possible, although the field is tricky and needs a lot of reasoning and sound judgment in order 'to separate the wheat from the chaff', as my own communicators have said.

Our Initiation in Instrumental Transcommunication

A few years before I had discovered by chance, in a small bookseller in Lisbon, two books on Instrumental Transcommunication, which in my view were of such incredible content that I put them aside without passing judgment, but also without any enthusiasm, not taking them very seriously for the fear of discovering one day that it was all to do with science fiction or speculative futurism. I believe this statement will give the readers the measure of my ignorance on the subject, since I even ignored at the time the existence of Friedrich Jürgenson's and Konstantin Raudive's works.

The books that puzzled me so much were Hildegard Schäfer's, *Ponte entre o Aqui e o Além* (1993, Portuguese translation of the original in German) and Théo Locher and Maggie Harsch-Fischbach's, *Les Contacts vers l'Au-delà à l'aide de moyens techniques existent!* (1995 French translation of the 1989 original in German). The latter particularly impressed me because of the reports of the amazing contacts and revolutionary content of the messages purportedly received from higher beings. This information was of such nature that if it were true it would mean a paradigm shift of such magnitude as to radically change the behavior of humanity.

I informed my friends of everything I had 'discovered' about ITC, although using all possible caution so as not to create expectations in them about the existence of something that could bring them back into life, so to speak, only to find out that they had no grounds for hope because the phenomenon either did not exist or the whole thing was mere futuristic speculation, a tale of such bad taste that it could seriously affect bereaved people.

I should explain that in Spain (as in other Southern European countries) there is no tradition of consulting a medium to contact the deceased and so this method is not normally used by serious-minded people. Such supposed 'spirit' contacts are normally claimed by unscrupulous self-proclaimed mediums who take advantage of the weak minded through the use of classical methods of commercial marketing and psychological manipu- lation, as we see in the abundant tawdry advertisements in newspapers and magazines. The subject is also referred to in the context of TV programs of doubtful quality, where it mainly addresses predicting the future of celebrities' relationships.

I remember we used to discuss the subject of ITC in those faraway days without taking it seriously because, as we would argue, if such a possibility existed how was it possible that all the TV programs, newspapers, etc. all over the world would not spread the news about the most important thing on Earth, i.e., the contact with another world and the deceased? This seemed so obvious to us that we became skeptical about the reality of the communications reported in those books. This recurrent question, which incidentally still appears valid today, made us shrug our shoulders and shake our heads not knowing what to think. But, on the other hand, there were the names of scientists, theologians, acoustic engineers, technicians, academicians of all areas of knowledge associated with the subject as our newly- acquired friend, Carlos Fernández, an electronic technician, and himself a theoretical expert on the phenomenon, used to tell us.

We Seek the Advice of a Jesuit priest

One day I had the idea of suggesting to my friends that we seek the advice of a Spanish Jesuit priest, Father José Maria Pilón (Pilón, 1996), a highly respected man and an expert on the paranormal, as well as a well known author on the subject. I managed to book an interview with the aged priest in Madrid, where he lives, and the three of us went to the capital with great expectations. We had lunch with Father Pilón in a pleasant restaurant in Madrid, and over an extended, relaxed and delicious meal, so typical of Spanish culture, we had the opportunity of telling him the whole story and the parents' despair. He listened to them with compassion and the wisdom with which many years of listening to and studying similar stories had endowed him. To our great surprise, at the end of a three-hour meeting, Father Pilón said, 'In my opinion the most suitable thing for you would be to try and establish contact with your son through ITC.' We had not mentioned anything about ITC to him in view of the fact that we had previously decided not to influence him in any way.

We Start Our Experimentation

We came back to Galicia full of enthusiasm and feeling much more secure as a result of Father Pilón's support for the 'adventure' of experimenting with ITC. We decided to try it, with the precious help of Carlos Fernández and his theoretical knowledge of the practical aspects of the methods involved – an area that fascinates him.

Those were exciting times, full of doubts, fears of 'doing something wrong', puzzlement at the apparent simplicity of the procedures and a lot of mixed emotions difficult to describe when a group of laypeople begin attempting to contact a transcendental dimension. Furthermore, at the back of our minds, I think we did not seriously envisage the possibility of seeing one day our cumbersome, naïve endeavors become successful. It would be too good to be true! Nevertheless, we were determined to carry on with our experiments.

Since we had no idea about the technical procedures involved, simple as they are when you know them, Carlos Fernández' advice was truly instrumental in the whole process.

I am not a technically oriented person and my other two friends had no great experience of technical matters, either. I had not touched a computer before and was not even at ease with a tape recorder. The whole matter seemed particularly bizarre to us because we thought that such a complex communication – the unimaginable contact with another world – surely needed highly complex methods and procedures. I am sure that even Carlos Fernández was a little perplexed by the simplicity of the whole system when we started to put into practice his knowledge of the 'classical' methods. To be very frank, Carlos Fernández, although knowledgeable and very attracted to the idea of ITC phenomena, was doubtful, as he confessed to us, of their authenticity. For him, as a technician, the whole thing was 'impossible'. In his excellent survey of ITC phenomena (see e.g. Fernández, 2006) Carlos admits to this, especially the DRV that, as he puts it, 'If I had not witnessed and experienced them myself I would not have believed that this phenomenon was real.'

We started to experiment with the images using the so-called Schreiber method of feedback. Briefly, it is a feedback loop created by the filming with a video camera of random light image/s (on a TV set screen or computer monitor) created by the zoom of the video camera connected through a cable to the TV or computer and focused on the screen in the most adequate position to produce light spots preferably in the shape of a tunnel, and operated to continually film the oscillating light effects. This is a closed circuit because the video-camera is directly connected to the TV set or computer and the captured image is projected onto the screen through the cable connection to be continuously filmed and again projected and again filmed in a loop.

Later on, through the projection onto the screen/monitor of the filmed images frame by frame (a slow process that demands a lot of attention), we can examine what was recorded by the video camera.

We bought a small computer and a video camera expressly for this purpose. Immediately, with the first attempts at psychoimages, we got what we thought were positive results. They were not extremely sharp images but they were sufficiently clear for us to perceive human faces, profiles and images of animals.

The first images we could compare with the photos of the deceased were apparently of Dae, an old Great Dane dog I had found starved almost to death, ill and abandoned. I had treated and taken care of her until her death about a year and a half before our experiment. Her big black and white spots, the shape of her head, her pointedly cut ears appeared visibly on the screen contrasting against the background of random spots. However, we were extremely intent on perfection and were looking for photographic quality, having decided when we started that we would reject any image that could not be compared point by point with the image of the deceased while alive. Above all, we did not want to deceive ourselves, and this is certainly an extremely important precaution that anybody who wishes to experiment with ITC should take. But I think we stretched our parameters too far because those first images could have been duly compared to the dog's photographs while alive. I now regret that we did not pay them the attention they deserved. There were other images of animals, amongst them one of a dog that could be attributed to a different deceased abandoned dog that I had also sheltered in my house. There were images of people, some of them in what appeared to be historical attire, but they were not the photographic imprints we were looking for, and so we directed our experiments towards the EVP.

Experimenting with EVP or Voices on Tape

We worked in a small room in my house that I had put aside for the purpose of experimenting and decided to meet as regularly as we could, at least once a week. That small room has been my ITC studio ever since.

We started our regular work on the very last days of October 1997 and met regularly without fail, week after week. The bereaved couple would come to my house from a little town near

La Coruña, some 150 km away, while Carlos came from just 30km from my house.

From the very beginning, our attitude was one of utmost seriousness and respect. We rigorously took notice of every single occurrence or noise produced in the environment during our experimentation and kept total silence throughout the time we recorded. All little noises from a sudden click in the radio to a slight cough of one of us would be registered in our experimentation log. We also wrote down our questions beforehand as well as the date, hour, phase of the moon, weather conditions, psychological mood of each one of us, and other little incidents we thought might be of interest. We used two radios tuned to the static noise between stations (the so-called 'white noise') – one SW radio and an AM normal radio tuned to what is called by ITC experimenters the 'Jürgenson wave', around 1500 KHz, because this is the frequency that he mostly used. A few weeks later, Carlos transformed a small portable radio into a 'broadband' receiver and that too we added to the equipment. We used to sit on the floor and the two, later three, radios produced the acoustic carrier that we normally used as the background noise for our recordings.

The questions (two or three from each of us) were asked in our native languages – my friend Lola spoke in Galician, Carlos Fernández in Spanish and I in Portuguese. My friend's husband was never really interested in the subject; it did not appeal to him. Actually, he never got involved in the experimentation and his presence was mainly to support his wife rather than truly experiment with ITC. After some time, he even stopped coming because she now seemed much better and was able to do the driving back and forth on her own. When we finished the recording we used to have dinner in my house sometimes late at night, around 11.00 pm.

We started the ITC work at the end of October and for two and a half months we meticulously followed this routine. The three of us – Carlos, Lola and I – would carefully listen to the tape and write down in our log any little sound that had not been produced or heard by us during our recording. At least a couple of times we noticed odd sounds on the tape like sighs or muffled breathing that sounded very near the microphone. Such phenomena are described in ITC literature and it is reported that they can sometimes happen before proper voices appear recorded on the tapes. We had now bought more books on ITC and were, therefore, alerted to these apparently anomalous occurrences.

But as had happened with the psychoimages, we decided not to accept anything other than proper coherent voices as evidence; hence, we were not convinced and did not pay special attention to these anomalous sounds. We used to also get what sounded like knocks, some of them quite loud, which had not been produced in the experimentation area or by the radio. My house is located in a secluded spot, high in the hills over the ocean and there are no other houses in the immediate vicinity. It is surrounded by a very large garden of 3,000 sq. meters and any noises can be easily identified.

We used two tape recorders – one of them belonged to Lola and the other one to me. Sometimes those strange knocks could only be heard on my tape, sometimes on both, sometimes louder in mine but we could not detect any voices.

The First EVP Voice

On 17th of January 1998, we decided to use a radio emission in German as acoustic carrier (background noise). One single voice could be heard announcing what seemed to be the news. This was one of the very few times when we used a radio emission in a foreign language as background source of noise. We shall discuss acoustic carriers in detail in the chapter that deals with the experimentation techniques.

Interestingly, we did not use foreign radio emissions more

than two or three times altogether because our preoccupation with precision and strict adherence to a rigorous protocol in order to avoid self-deception led us to the conclusion that it was 'safer' not to use them. Nevertheless, they are excellent acoustic supports used by a number of experimenters, but in my opinion are also susceptible of creating undesirable confusion.

Readers might be curious about the type of questions we used to ask during our experimental sessions. The truth is that we would ask almost everything. Naturally, Lola inquired mainly about her son; Carlos liked to ask technical questions about the equipment and I used to ask a whole range of questions from the adequateness of the frequencies and positions of the radios in the room, to the living conditions and descriptions of the next world. On that specific day of January my question had been the following: 'Is the reason why we have had no positive results so far to protect us from negative influences?' To our amazement and delight, upon rewinding the tape, we clearly heard a pretty loud 'Sim' in Portuguese, uttered by a completely different voice from that of the radio announcer during a pause in the German words.

This 17th of January marked the great shift in our work. From there on, the EVP replies to our questions became quite frequent and often of very good acoustic quality. They were apparently uttered by a number of feminine and masculine different voices and were normally in Portuguese with a few in Galician and in Spanish. This development was a huge step forward for us and a tremendous incentive. In view of it, we decided, with the exception of Carlos who never seemed interested in individual experimentation, to carry on with our own experimental work on other days besides our weekly meetings which, of course, we did not stop.

I admit that the experience of receiving EVP replies was such a thrilling event in my life that I used to experiment on my own almost every day or at least three times a week. When we worked together, we experimented with different acoustic carriers besides the 'white noise' of the radios – commercial tapes with natural sounds, such as the shrieks of joy of dolphins and whales, the murmur of the sea, instrumental and relaxing music, Gregorian chants, etc. On my own I usually preferred to use the 'white noise' of the old valve SW radio that I had acquired in the meantime, together with the 'white noise' produced by the AM radio tuned to the 'Jürgenson wave', around 1500 KHz, and the little portable radio that Carlos had transformed into a 'broadband' receiver.

The first EVP, after that splendid first 'Sim', answered my question on how could I, from my side, contribute to the improvement of the contacts, with the word 'Contact'. Another reply to a similar question was, 'You can help the communication: it means your work,' in the odd syntactic construction that characterizes some ITC voices. I suppose we can conclude from these two replies that the persistent, tireless endeavors of the experimenter (which are obviously a reflection of his or her interest and motivation) to contact the next world constitute a positive input in the establishing of the famous 'Bridge' of contact which Friedrich Jürgenson and later other researchers made abundant references to, as we will discuss in the next chapters.

The communicators frequently used the word 'Bem' (Well [Right or correct] in English) instead of 'Sim' (Yes) for affirmative replies, and at the beginning of the contacts, they would also apparently reply with the strong taps or knocks I mentioned before instead of using the words 'Sim' or 'Não' respectively for the affirmative and negative. Puzzled by this, I asked if they were using the code of the Spiritist/Spiritualist sessions – one knock for 'No' and two knocks for 'Yes' – to which they replied 'Bem' (right). One evening I asked if they could hear me and the low EVP said 'They can hear; impossible.' This, I interpreted as information about the difficulty of communicating that day and indeed no more voices were recorded.

Looking at my diary of those first months of 1998, I verify that although there were replies in all different phases of the moon, there is a remarkable disparity in positive results. We had the most when the moon was waxing, followed by a slight drop on the full moon; there were fewer at the new moon but there was a considerable difference in the period of the waning moon when the least results were obtained.

Extraordinary things happened every day in those first months when voices would mysteriously appear on a blank audio tape, some of them as loud and clear as a normal voice speaking to me in the same room. The taped voices are indeed a marvel to hear, something 'unbelievable' that one has to witness personally, to see them happen in front of one's own eyes and to hear them with one's own ears, to fully realize their magical nature. But the most thrilling events were still to come! It all began one late afternoon at sunset as we will see in the next chapter.

Chapter 4

More Extensive Personal Experiences and Contact with 'Rio do Tempo'

The First Direct Radio Voice (DRV)

It was the end of the beautiful afternoon of the 11th of March, 1998 a date that will be in my heart and in my mind forever. A bright light still glimmered on the sea and the foliage as a result of the early morning rain. The air was pleasant and mild because a warm sun had been shining throughout the day. And suddenly the most astounding event in my whole life took place! A masculine voice that seemed to shout a reply to the question I had just asked during my EVP experimental session came out directly from the loudspeaker of the old valve radio! A new, totally unexpected development had happened – contact through the DRV method; something any experimenter, or anyone inter-ested in the subject, can read about in any of the many works of the already extensive literature on this discipline but never expects it to happen to him or her.

It was a sunny day of a winter that was more like spring. I remember looking through the window of my studio and thinking that the light at the end of the day looked unusually clear and brilliant. It was 8:15 pm and I was alone at home with the dogs. The usual radios of that period of my research were connected – an old valve radio tuned into the 14 MHz of the SW band, an ordinary portable Sony radio of no special quality tuned into the 'Jürgenson frequency' at around 1500 KHz, and the broad-band radio (the description of which will be given in Chapter 11), which Carlos Fernández had prepared for us. The moon was waxing.

I sat alone on the floor of my little studio preparing for one of my solo experimental sessions, as we had decided to do, and I asked the first question of the evening: 'Are we really communicating with the Landell Group and with Carlos de Almeida?' At this point I should explain why I mentioned these two names. I had learned through a Portuguese friend, who was much better informed on ITC and other contacts with the Beyond than me, that in the next dimension of life a group (composed primarily of Portuguese and Brazilians, and known as the Landell Group) was supposed to exist and that they contacted our world through Instrumental Transcommunication from Rio do Tempo Station.

Father Roberto Landell de Moura, now deceased, had been a famous Brazilian Catholic priest and scientist, inventor of the wave transmitter and other highly advanced devices that preceded the radio. He was pioneer in the transmission of the human voice, and in 1899 did a successful public experiment in São Paulo with his wave transmitter, managing to contact his receptor placed some 8 km away. He got Brazilian and US patents for his inventions called the 'Wave Transmitter', the 'Wireless Telephone' and the 'Wireless Telegraph'. From the patents, it can be inferred that at such an early epoch Landell de Moura already thought of short waves to facilitate the transmissions. He was believed to work in close cooperation, in the next world, with a Portuguese communicator called Carlos de Almeida, apparently very active in ITC work, and other figures of Brazilian, Portuguese and African origin. Thus, on this bright evening of March 11th, wondering whether the important number of good quality EVP replies we were receiving by then were coming from an organized, knowledgeable source, I spontaneously asked this question.

After a lapse of a few seconds, a loud masculine voice suddenly erupted from the loudspeaker of the old valve radio, obviously speaking to me, echoing in the total silence of my house, for the dogs were all quiet at that hour. My surprise was indescribable and I felt a tremendous inner shock. To this day I admire my composure, my *sang-froid*, which I did not know I possessed, for I was able to react coherently and to speak (I have to say that I rather shouted) to this voice, which in reply continued addressing me. And as abruptly as it had come, the voice vanished.

The speech was quite long and consisted of a number of sentences (this first DRV is included in the CD that accompanies the book) but at the time, under the shock, I could only understand 'difícil' (difficult) and 'outro mundo' (another world). When the whole thing suddenly stopped and only the soft buzz of the radio could be heard again, my first impression was that I would not be able to move. My legs felt empty and unable to support my body, my hands and my chin shook uncontrollably and the rest of my body felt as numb and lifeless as a dummy. I was almost paralyzed with the shock.

With great effort, I got up from the armchair where I was sitting and reached out to the telephone, shaking and feeling like shouting for a long time to release the incredible emotion I was feeling. I called Carlos Fernández, my sole help and advisor in those days. Carlos was in Santiago de Compostela at a conference but fortunately he answered his mobile phone. I told him what had happened and asked him to come to my house immediately for I could not stand the incredible excitement and emotion and wanted him to listen to the recording. As always Carlos reacted prudently. He asked if I was sure the voice was speaking to me, tried to calm me down and said he could not come that evening since he could not leave the conference of which he was one of the organizers but that he would come the next day, as early as possible. And so, I remained sitting on the floor of my lounge next to the telephone for a long time, shaking and unable to think or to speak. Perhaps I could also say that I was scared but the word scared is not appropriate or enough to define what I felt. I find that very intense emotions are always difficult to put into words, for words come from the intellect and the human intellect is not sufficiently vast, sensitive and open to be able to describe feelings of a very special and unusual nature. Perhaps my most intense feeling was one of incredulity.

I was not able to sleep the whole night. I rolled in bed from side to side and could not control the shaking that by now affected mostly my chin. The voice had sounded very strange and strident, as if shouting from the bottom of a tunnel, making a tremendous effort to speak, and I suppose, in those crucial hours that followed this extraordinary and unexpected development, all the preconceived ideas implanted by centuries of macabre ideas and traditions about death must have played an important part in my reaction. My mind and my body were on fire. Those hours and most of the next day, until Carlos arrived in the afternoon, seemed eternal. I still could not control the trembling, which had by now become intermittent.

Carlos and I listened to the recording but we could not understand with certainty the content of all the utterances besides 'difícil' and 'outro mundo'. Nevertheless, we realized, without doubt, that something amazing had happened. It was plainly obvious that the voice was speaking to me, and even Carlos, always cautious, reserved and moderate, understood that without any doubt. It could certainly not have been a radio transmission, for radio announcers do not suspend their delivery while the listener is speaking, neither do they shout as if to make themselves more clearly understood, and they do not normally speak of 'another world'.

In the next couple of days, with the help of a young friend (the son of an important political figure in the Spanish Administration of that period, who possesses superb hearing capabilities), we were able to understand the whole of the bizarre speech from that memorable evening. It said:

Estamos a ouvir tudo, queremos saber do mundo, queremos ouvir **vuestras cosas** (Spanish); agora vamos contar convosco, oferecer o que é justo! **Eu não fui este quem falasse** (a very odd syntactic construction in Portuguese) mas **supongo** (Spanish) que você tenha feito alguma **pregunta** (Spanish)! Isto é muito e muito difícil! Outro mundo!

(Literal translation: 'We are listening to everything. We want to know about the world. We want to hear your things. Now we are going to count on you, to offer what is just! I was not the one who spoke, but I suppose you have made a question! This is very and very difficult! Another world!').

Our entire little group was in complete agreement with this interpretation. It is important to explain that our little group was constituted of people with no special hearing proficiency. Among them I was perhaps the most 'intent listener' because the other two had no particular interest in the listening process, and also no especially good physiological hearing aptitude, according to their own statements.

Indeed, the process of hearing can be a complex one. When you have to listen to a recorded audio track (e.g. in EVP experimentation) for 30 minutes or more without shifting your attention from the sound, the listening process can become a tricky business. The anomalous voices may be there but you may not hear them because they are faint and you cannot concentrate consistently on every single sound without changing the focus of your attention, or they mix with the background noise and become blurred, distorted, etc. Concentration is the key to good hearing, especially in EVP experimentation. The great pioneer of EVP, Friedrich Jürgenson, commented on this issue, saying,

We should not ignore that the art of concentrated listening is a relatively rare gift. It is one that can be learned under certain conditions with much patience. Basically, we are dealing with an introspective concentration capability to focus exclusively on the sounds or frequencies that need to be researched without allowing oneself to be distracted and mistaken by simultaneous interference. (Jürgenson, 1967)

In my view this is a perfect evaluation of the situation.

Nevertheless, this first DRV was loud and not excessively mixed with the radio buzz; the most important reason for my initial difficulty of comprehension was the fact that it was so totally unexpected that it very much startled me. It put me almost in a state of shock and, under these circumstances, how can anybody understand precisely what was said? Furthermore, the voice made a little speech; it did not simply reply 'Yes' or 'No' to my question. The voice conveyed its own message and to some extent the content of the voice's speech was at first sight not a direct answer to my question. The voice said the things the communicator wanted to express which were not in direct connection to my simple question, although they were about my question.

This constitutes an important factor that can be corroborated in ordinary everyday life if we consider the well known social situation when someone enters a room where a conversation is taking place between a group of people, and as the newcomer arrives he or she immediately hears a word or couple of words, pronounced loudly and clearly by somebody in the room but cannot understand them. Normally that person will ask, 'What is it that you said?' and when the explanation comes, the usual remark will be 'Oh yeah, of course, but I had not heard the question.' In a conversation, the relationship of words to that which has been said previously is a factor that greatly facilitates the clear comprehension of what is said.

This rule applies to normal as well as to anomalous voices, which are of a more delicate nature, not so much because they are psychophonic voices, but very simply because they are recorded voices and often the recording was not done with particularly good equipment. Any normal recorded voice will not be very easy to understand if it is taken out of context and/or if the recording is slightly blurred. Indeed, in such a situation the matter becomes complicated to the point that sometimes I cannot understand what I have said on the tapes and have to go over and over my own voice to understand the question or the remark I made a few years ago. Add to this some, although not excessive, background noise (the buzz produced by the radios was quite soft) and we have a complex acoustic situation! Naturally, some voices are clearer than others, for ITC contacts do not obey rules – at least our rules.

Needless to say that the event which took place in my house on March 11, 1998 at sunset was the reason for tremendous excitement for all of us, and very particularly for me who had directly participated in it. This time even Carlos Fernández, who is a quiet and not very effusive person, got thrilled and, as he says in his latest book (Fernández, 2006), he was really 'stunned' because at the back of his mind this was something that could not happen. Our friend and colleague, Lola, was even more ignorant than I of the rarity of this situation because she had heard or read nothing about the new techniques to attempt transcendental contacts through electronic media. I had read a couple of reports on the DRV, and although I did not really question the veracity of those testimonies, I suppose in some way my mind took them to be a kind of fairy tale, something fantastic that might happen to a couple of people in the whole world but that would not certainly happen to me. To hear that bizarre voice resonating in the silence of my house was as if an inconceivable miracle had happened in front of my eyes. My goodness, the dead speaking through a radio!

A few days later, when I was able to reason again, my awe became boundless! To tell the truth, for a period I found myself having to listen to the recording over and over again to believe that this had really happened to me. When I realized the magnitude of the situation, the state of shock I had experienced slowly gave way to an overwhelming sense of joy and gratitude towards those who had been able to pierce through the veil of the Unknown to reach to us from another level of reality in such an impressive way. Tears would come to my eyes every time I thought about it. I felt immensely proud, as I still feel today, to be involved in an enterprise of unparalleled significance.

More Direct Radio Voices Followed

On the 14th of March the moon was already full and our little group assembled for another experimental session. Again, the radio voices appeared but this time they were less perceptible and their acoustic quality much inferior to what it had been the first time. The clearest utterance said, 'Grupo Testemunho do Sol!' (Group Testimony of the Sun!) in reply to my request of identification. Something very interesting happened during this second DRV. My friend Lola, who was also present on this occasion, requested of the communicators, since the voices were quite faint, 'Can you please reply to us more loudly?' and to this they replied lowly but clearly 'Não podemos, a gente fala de outro mundo...' (We cannot, we speak from another world). Once again the answer reflects the enormous difficulties involved in the communication process. For instance, a communicator from Rio do Tempo Station once said suddenly to me in the middle of a DRV communication 'Contacto bom é difícil...' (Good contact is difficult) and they have repeated similar statements innumerable times.

On the 29th of the same month, in the presence of Carlos Fernández, Mukesh Godyal, who then worked in my house, and myself, contact by DRV was again established (at 19H15h) and it lasted for a very long time although quite less clear than the first day. When we turned off the radios at 22H15h, the same masculine voice that identified itself as belonging to *Platão*, continued to try and reply to our questions and comments but most of it was practically unintelligible. In any event, the astounding thing about this contact was that it lasted for three hours, although interspersed with pauses. This contact was one of the longest so far received, and some interesting messages were clear enough to be understood without difficulty. They said things such as 'Há um abismo no outro mundo…' (There is an abyss in the other world…). One of the most frequently repeated sentences was 'Outro mundo' (Another world) uttered not only in response to my insistent questions as to who was speaking on that particular day, but spontaneously repeated several times by the communicators too. In reply to the same question from me they also said: 'Os mortos falam' (The dead speak).

Another striking feature of this incredible evening was the emotional impact it had upon me – as anyone who listens to the tape will readily understand – by virtue of the fact that the recording is full of EVP (sentences not heard directly by any of us present in the room at the time) spoken by several masculine and feminine voices that differed from the voice that was communicating simultaneously through DRV. Sometimes loud, sometimes faint, these voices commented on what Carlos and I were saying or on what was happening in the room. It was as if a group of invisible people were there together with us, witnessing everything that was happening. In fact, maybe they really were there because, in reply to my frequent questions as to whether or not they could hear me, they twice said in a rather husky voice, 'We are listening to everything, we are here with you.' If they really were there in the studio, that might be one of the factors that contributed to the impressive number of EVPs recorded during that particular communication. That and perhaps the tremendous excitement and emotion from both sides – ours and the communicators' – also played a role in it.

It was on the same evening of the 29th of March 1998 that one of the most remarkable EVP voices I have ever heard was registered on the last of the two full tapes that we recorded that evening. There is a very interesting story behind this particular voice that I will briefly explain. As I said above, Carlos Fernández was in my house that evening and together we were participating in the contacts that occurred. Initially, as I think I explained previously, I was in the habit of almost shouting during DRV communications. As this particular communication was one of the very first DRV contacts I ever received, and because it lasted for such a long time it became an extremely emotional event for me. When I listen to the tape now I can hear myself calling with all my heart for contacts with my deceased father and brother, with my beloved grandmother, with my beloved Doberman dogs, with my dearest deceased friends. My emotional level was obviously particularly high as I realized for the first time that my deceased dearly loved ones, whom I greatly missed, might be listening to us, and understandably this was an extraordinary revelation.

Although I am not an atheist, I do not follow Spiritism, Spiritualism or any other religion, and in addition I have had a very rational upbringing. In consequence, the awe of something that seemed totally impossible until the ITC contacts commenced was overwhelming and I had difficulty in coping with it. I spontaneously cried and thanked the communicators and God for the 'impossible miracle' so unexpectedly offered to me. Indeed, on several occasions it seemed that my dear family members, whom I used to call frequently, were trying to reply directly to me, and on other occasions the communicator could be heard saying for instance '... falamos com ele' (... we speak with him) when I addressed my beloved deceased dog Surya. There was an intense interaction throughout the whole recording that made it particularly moving.

Naturally, the drama of the situation led to my habit of almost yelling; a habit that became particularly noticeable that evening. At a certain point, Carlos said to me, 'Do not shout. Why do you shout?' To this I replied by laughing and by asking the communicators if they had heard what Carlos had said. I excused myself by explaining that I shouted because I had the impression that they could hear me better if I did. Carlos laughed too and said, 'Well, speaking loudly or softly has nothing to do with it,' [i.e. with whether the communicators could hear me better or not]. Immediately after Carlos finished his sentence, a very clear, loud, feminine EVP voice, that sounded rather similar, although not identical, to my own voice, could be heard upon replaying the tape, distinctly or more distinctly than our own voices, saying 'Claro que não tem nada que ver, a ilusão que temos nós, eles não me podem ouvir tem de ser através do mar' (Of course it has nothing to do with it. The same illusion that we have. They cannot hear me. It has to be through the sea'). This was an obvious confirmation of Carlos' remark on the fact that shouting or speaking softly had nothing to do with the communicators being able to hear me.

The questions raised by this beautiful, enigmatic EVP voice (beautiful by virtue of its clarity and intelligibility) are many, but we will discuss them in another chapter. It is enough to say here that, as I mentioned at the beginning of this chapter, the first DRV voice that I received also seemed to be shouting, and that perhaps explains the reference on this occasion to 'the same illusion that we have'. A humorous note was struck at the same time by a masculine voice, this time a DRV voice that commented, immediately before I asked the communicators if they had heard Carlos telling me not to shout, 'Nós não somos surdos!' (We are not deaf!) There were other relevant EVP voices on this occasion, for instance the feminine, melodious, very beautiful voice – apparently the same voice that would later speak about the dogs in a few instances – that said 'Oh bébé!' (Oh baby!) apparently referring to my live Doberman dog, Lady, one of Surya's and Nisha's puppies, who was nearby during this recording session and whom I used to call 'Bébé' to express the immense tenderness I felt for her.

There are, on my tapes, several references to the dogs that include their names, and several voices that address them directly (both EVP and DRV voices), and on this occasion another feminine voice spoke the name of one of my deceased dogs, Nisha (Lady's mother), twice. The rather long EVP sentence continued with a totally different voice as of an old lady that sobbed and uttered loudly, clearly and unmistakably in German 'Ich war medioker!' (I was mediocre!), and there was even the sound of a little bird singing. When I asked the communicators if they had a little bird with them, an EVP voice replied 'Sim' (Yes). There was also a gentle, hushed masculine voice that very much resembled my father's voice that called 'Belinha!' Belinha is the pet name my whole family called me throughout my early life, and that is still used today by my sister and by my nieces.

On the 30th of March, around 21H00, while I was alone in my studio, contact was again established through the DRV, and the communication of that evening (of which there is a short extract on the CD that comes with the book) was very clear but not as loud as the first one. I called this beautiful communication, during which I tried not to speak in order not to disturb the recording, the *Power of Infinity*, for it says among many other things '… and I feel a little heather; and I feel another color, I feel my power of infinity; the unconscious of God covers all. Always think of our world; whoever thinks of our world reduces the distances…' I live on the top of a small hill in a house overlooking the bay of Vigo and indeed everywhere around my house there is lots of heather, a plant that I am particularly fond of. The voice had also said before the above transcription '… and I feel a very English collie…'. Actually, in the garden of my house playing with the other dogs, while I was recording, there was Red, an abandoned collie that I had rescued some time before. This is a good example of the type of perception that this particular communicator, who identified himself as Filipe, seems to have – firstly the masculine voice says 'I feel', not I see. I once asked my communicators if they could see me and their reply to this was, 'It means a lot of work! [for them to be able to see us]'. Nevertheless, on another occasion, another voice replied to a similar question with 'Only some can [see our world].' The question as to the extent to which the communicators can 'see' our world, therefore, still remains open. It is interesting to note that in the above quotation, Filipe says '...I feel my power of infinity...' a beautiful expression that is perhaps intended to describe the expansion of consciousness that is achieved by the beings in his world. He also seems to tie the feeling of his power of infinity to his feeling of another color: '...and I feel another color, I feel my power of infinity...'

Apparently, the concept of 'color' is used by Filipe in a very different way to ours. Would this be the influence of his own higher world, or plane, as Frederic Myers calls it? This last possibility is well worth considering. Frederic Myers – a great figure in the field of survival research and one of the three founders of the British S.P.R., who is said to be the deceased communicator of what I consider to be one of the most impressive series of messages concerning the nature of the afterlife received through a human medium (Cummins, 1932) – does in fact refer to what he calls 'The Plane of Colour.' He tells us that

> Existence in this state is not governed by the senses. It is more directly controlled by the mind. It is still an existence in form, and therefore an existence in substance... This many-coloured world is nourished by light, and life in a greater purity vibrates at an unimaginable speed. The souls, who dwell within the first zone, realise that with increased consciousness they have gained a far greater sensitivity... (pp. 33, 57).

It all seems to correspond to Filipe feeling another color and his power of infinity. 'The Plane of Colour' is classified by Myers as the fourth stage of existence, while the Earth is the first one. Myers' description may explain why Filipe refers to color, apparently in a very different sense from the way in which we use the term. For him, 'color' seems to be an all-embracing concept intimately connected to 'feeling'. The term 'feeling' also seems to carry a much broader meaning for Filipe than it does for us. As Myers puts it, '…with increased consciousness they have gained a far greater sensitivity.' It all seems to indicate that Filipe is at a higher plane of existence corresponding to a higher plane of consciousness that Myers calls 'The Plane of Colour'.

I have extensively quoted and made use of Myers' alleged information because much of what Rio do Tempo communicators have said in several instances seems to corroborate it but, nevertheless, we should also keep in mind what Myers says about human mediumship:

> You must remember that a medium is rarely a mere medium. He should be called an 'interpreter'. It is an interpretation, not a literal statement that is conveyed to you through him.

At the request of Sir Oliver Lodge, who had asked Myers to confirm the authorship of the Cummins' scripts, he goes on to say, through Lodge's deceased son and another medium, referring to the content of *The Road to Immortality* that:

> In a general way he had managed to get through what he wanted; though he admitted it was difficult, and he couldn't be sure that it was always exact, but still on the whole he was willing to pass it as fairly representing what he had intended to say.
> (In Foreword by Oliver Lodge, Cummins ibid, 1932)

While the deformation caused by the intervention of the human mind does not seem to apply to the communications received through ITC, we should still bear in mind that the communicators are necessarily limited by our own concepts when they wish to communicate with us. Since they have to use our words, which are the direct result of human thought, it will be practically impossible for them to give an accurate picture of their world through the use of human language, which naturally is only apt to describe our own level of reality. When they speak through ITC, a process that apparently does not directly use the human mind but has to use human language because we would not be able to comprehend what falls outside our own conceptual world, they still have to deal with the important limitations that are surely involved when communicating from one dimension of reality to another, if they are to offer us the opportunity of grasping even a part of their meaning.

If we ponder on the restrictions attendant upon the communications from the afterlife, especially the insurmountable ones that occur as a result of the differences between our limited and their increased reach of consciousness, as well as of the complexity of the information the communicators seek to transmit (such as details of the conditions and characteristics of their world), we ought to approach the whole issue with humility. I think we have to consider that many of the details given to us by the communicators should, in many instances, be taken symbolically rather than literally. Yet, we have to keep in mind that the symbols we may envisage through their descriptions will still be our own symbols and those can only fall within the reach of our consciousness. Although this is an insuperable difficulty, it is important that we are aware of its existence in order to keep our mind open to all possibilities, even the ones that seem 'impossible' to us.

Indeed, we cannot pretend to understand the many symbolic expressions and metaphors that the communicators use plentifully, and perhaps we should not even try because in that there is a big risk of making mistakes and presenting things as something they are not. This would be particularly harmful, since the information and concepts that reach us from those more advanced dimensions should naturally be taken very seriously and such being the case, 'interpretations' should be extremely cautious. They should be offered as the subjective understanding of a particular experimenter, not as the given truth of the next world. There must be many 'truths' in the next world according to the level of consciousness of who communicates and conveys the information, and consequently extrapolations should be avoided.

Many other DRV contacts followed, and during that period voices that came directly from the loudspeaker of the radio could be heard in my house almost every evening. As usual, I asked a lot of questions and inquired also about more practical issues such as the identification of the speakers, the best time for the communications, the best equipment, etc. When I could clearly understand the replies, I would accordingly either change or continue with what I was doing, thus modestly contributing from my side to the improvement of the channel of communication as much as I could.

The identity of the speakers seems to be difficult information to obtain, and although I received a good number of replies to my questions that yielded personal names and surnames, some of them totally unknown to me, I also have others when an apparently superior entity intervenes to recommend that names be not given. For example, when a voice identified itself with my father's name, it was immediately followed by another voice that said, 'You don't have to say that [his name], only Rio do Tempo!' You can listen to this voice on the CD that comes with the book. I assume this situation must be related to the concept of the Group-Soul which seems to be a strong reality in the next world, as we shall discuss in subsequent chapters.

Chapter 5

Identification of Rio do Tempo Station

The Identification of Rio do Tempo Station

In October of the same year of 1998, there was another extraordinary breakthrough. By that time I had got into the strict habit of experimenting almost every evening on my own with the hope each time of hearing those extraordinary voices addressing me directly through the loudspeaker of my radio; a hope that was by now fulfilled so frequently that in some ways I was tempted to doubt my own ears. It was against all I understood of reality, and certainly against all known laws of science that I could not only hear such voices, but that they appeared to actually come and dialogue with me from another dimension, which I supposed was the next world. Did these voices add further proof that we survive physical death and can actually communicate with those still living on earth? I hardly dared hope that this might be the case.

My method each time I experimented was simply to tune my radios to the wavelengths mid-way between two transmitting stations, so that all I could hear was the hiss of random noise, commonly called 'white noise'. The volume was always set at a comfortable listening level.

On October 7 I turned the radios on as usual, and took my seat in front of them, ready to switch on my tape recorder should there be any voices. As usual, I tried to keep my mind clear and calm and not to wait too eagerly for the reception of the voices, although as I was receiving anomalous voices almost every evening, it was difficult not to expect them. Sometimes I even took my dinner into my studio in order to wait there for the voices and to record them as soon as they started. The voices would say things such as 'O amor é eterno, não tem tempo,' (Love is eternal, it has no time) and sometimes it was as if I could overhear conversations, as if the communicators were talking among themselves about technical procedures for improving the communications. I have, in fact, recordings for almost every day of that October. For example, in one of the recordings, a voice replies to a question of mine about the situation of animals in their world by informing me that they are all protected. This reply fully agrees with the communications received by other ITC researchers. For example, Gabriella Alvisi, the remarkable Italian experimenter, herself not particularly keen on the fate of animals as she confesses in her books, received the same information through DRV in the 1970/1980s (Alvisi, 1976, 1983).

But let me return to the breakthrough that occurred on October 7th. Having turned on the radios as usual and taken up my position in front of them, I heard, through the loudspeaker of the old valve radio, what sounded like one of the usual voices announce loudly and clearly and beyond question that the communication was coming from a 'station' that he referred to as 'Rio do Tempo Station'. His exact words were (in Portuguese) 'Falamos da Estação Rio do Tempo, vais ficar bem contente, aposto!' (We speak from Rio do Tempo Station; you will be really glad I bet!), and this was followed by 'Tu fala directamente...' (You speak [to them] directly...). The last sentence – you speak directly – also has a particular relevance because I had got into the habit of listening to my recordings the following day and reflecting on what had been said to then comment about it to the communicators. Hence, their instruction to me that I could 'speak directly!' filled me with boundless joy because I knew that from now on I would be speaking directly to Rio do Tempo Station, a station considered by leading investigators to be one of the most advanced centers for contacts between the next world and ours. Up to that time, although I had received some replies implying the communications were from Rio do Tempo, there had been no definite confirmation of the fact. In reply to my questions, asking specifically if they were speaking from Rio do Tempo Station, I had received comments such as 'Sim, o lugar é, é aqui!' (Yes, the place is, is here!), or 'Sim, aqui!' (Yes, it is here!), but that was as far as they had gone. Their remark this time, that 'you will be really glad...,' was particularly appropriate because my ignorance of who, evening after evening, was speaking to me directly from the loudspeaker of a radio was one of the things that left me feeling apprehensive and rather worried as to who might be contacting me, particularly as I was aware from the literature that there may be undesirable communicators (Fisher, 1990).

Obviously the communicators knew of my concerns and tried to put my mind at rest while at the same time giving me great joy, for I was very impressed by what I had learnt from other investigators, such as Senkowski (1995) and Locher and Harsch (1995), about the amazing contacts that had been received from Rio do Tempo (Zeitstrom in German and Timestream in English). Thus, I was immensely grateful to the mysterious beings behind those unbelievable voices emanating apparently from what they described simply as 'another world'.

Deceased Members of My Family Make Contact Through the DRV Method

Another landmark in my communications was the day when I heard a voice saying it was my grandmother. This happened almost one year after I received the first DRV, and communications from other members of my family soon followed – my father, my brother Luís who had suddenly died of a heart attack in 1996 at 45 years of age, and (as we shall see) even from Nisha, one of my beloved Doberman dogs.

In the two months or so between receiving the first EVP voice and the first DRV – two months during which so many anomalous voices had been recorded on the tapes – I frequently asked to speak with deceased members of my family, especially my father to whom I am very attached and who during his lifetime in our world had shown a number of impressive psychic abilities. My father, who was a Finance Ministry Senior Officer and from a highly conservative, traditional Portuguese family, had no background knowledge of the so-called 'paranormal', but from childhood he had had puzzling personal experiences that included such things as spontaneous and frequent Out of the Body Experiences (OBEs) and retro-cognition. These experiences used to disturb and worry him deeply because he did not understand them or even know that such things also happen to other people. The only sources of information on these unusual events available to him, in the small conservative town in one of the most 'closed' regions of Portugal in which we lived, was the *Reader's Digest* to which he subscribed. He used to order the special big editions with titles such as *The Encyclopedia of the Fantastic* and *Unknown Powers of the Mind* and *The Book of the Supernatural* published by the *Digest*, and would wait eagerly for their arrival. I fancy that some of these large volumes must still be in my parents' old house or in the home of my sister. Sadly, no one in our family really shared my father's interest – apart perhaps for my brother and myself, but we were only teenagers at the time and occupied with what seemed to us to be more pressing teenage issues.

Not surprisingly, in view of these facts, as soon as I began to receive ITC communications I assumed that if anyone could speak with me from the next world it would be my father, and I even went to the extent of complaining to the voices that I thought my father would speak more easily than anybody else, and did not understand the reason why he failed to do so. To this, one of the communicators responded (as an EVP message) 'That's what you assume!' I imagined that this meant that my supposition that my father was best placed to speak to me was incorrect.

However, one day I heard and clearly understood the voice of a communicator who identified herself as my beloved grandmother. This was one of the happiest experiences during my experimentation thus far. From then on I spoke with that voice on a number of occasions, and we had moving short dialogues about trivial things – in one of them we spoke about rosemary (a plant I am very fond of) in her world and she also told me that 'the house [her house in the next world] is so beautiful,' so much so in fact that 'it is something, even too much' (an excerpt from the conversation concerned is included in the CD). One day during a DRV communication, I became unable to speak, so overwhelmed was I by the emotion caused by the contacts, and my grandmother said in a soft voice, 'Belinha, don't you know how to speak with me any longer?'

My brother Luís also spoke with me through DRV, and on two occasions gave his full name 'Luís Cardoso'. Then at last my father João Cardoso spoke, pronouncing his name loudly and clearly a number of times (see CD). I find it appropriate to share with my readers that I now consider that he had, in fact, tried to speak with me from the very first months of the DRV, but the sounds I had heard resembled strange shouts, unpleasant guttural noises, as if produced by a rough machine, trying to convey some kind of speech that I was unable to properly decipher at the time. However, today, after I have had the training that comes with listening to anomalous voices for thousands of hours, I can identify hidden in the harsh noise words such as 'Está a falar teu pai!' (It is your father speaking!) Nevertheless, these earlier attempts had not produced a proper voice, just sounds suggestive of a human voice to a properly trained ear.

This brings me back to two major difficulties in ITC communications. Firstly, the communicators must themselves encounter major difficulties in producing comprehensible, human-sounding voices by means of the 'modulation of radio waves with thought' (as they describe their own method). Remember, one of the communicators emphasized on the very first day of my reception of DRV that 'this is very and very difficult!' and on other occasions they reiterated the difficulties of the process. Secondly, we investigators also face difficulties during the listening process as a result of the peculiar acoustic character-istics of the majority of ITC voices. To these two difficulties we should add that ITC voices have nothing in common with the so-called paranormal voices heard coming through entranced mediums (assuming such voices are genuine). These mediu-mistic voices are thought to be produced by a manipulation of the vocal organs of the medium him/herself, whereas ITC voices are seemingly produced through a manipulation of random radio waves, which must be a much more difficult process, as no human agency is directly involved as an intermediary, but the voices thus formed still have to sound as human voices – an indispensable requisite for our comprehension of them.

Commenting on the difficulties involved in the listening process, Friedrich Jürgenson very appropriately put it that: 'Most listeners [referring to the guests who joined him to listen to the voices] found it difficult to be relaxed and to concentrate at the same time.' When observing someone who is new to ITC listening to the voices, one is in fact able to recognize the extent to which our frantic modern way of life has damaged the ability to pay close attention. All too often, inexperienced listeners become restless, impatient and, as Jürgenson put it, prone to show the 'internal fragmentation ... typical of the condition of the soul in our day and age.' And he continues:

I notice that even my friends and associates sometimes have difficulty when listening to the tapes of recorded [ITC] voices, despite their open and positive attitude towards my research work. Most tire quickly and become impatient, especially when they do not understand the text immediately. When I tell them what is being said they are usually annoyed with themselves for not recognizing it right away. Most of them do not remember that I have many years of hard training [in listening] behind me, a fact that is of decisive importance. It was only the very loud and distinct recordings that were understood by all. (Jürgenson, 1967).

To Jürgenson's well-informed and wise observations I would add the fact that even if the voice signal is mixed with extraneous noise, as is the case in some DRV communications, such as the ones that I believe were my father's first attempts to speak, the signal will still be there. Perhaps it will not be immediately perceptible even to the trained ear, but the sophisticated electro-acoustic processing software now available can, nevertheless, identify that the voice is there. Furthermore, depending on the signal to noise ratio, it can even be instrumentally decoded through computing techniques at least partially, rendering possible in most cases an interpretation of what is being said (Gullà 2007).

Acoustic analysis of this kind, using software developed by the FBI and used by the police in both Europe and the USA for voice recognition in criminal investigations, requires specialized knowledge, but such software tools now make possible the proper scientific investigation of ITC voices. Sadly, the majority of parapsychologists know nothing of these recent and vitally important advances. Moreover, they also do not know that they do not know, and this is an even bigger problem!

I am convinced that 'the extremely difficult process of communication', as defined by the communicators, also needs to be learned and mastered by those who speak from the other side, and such practice must be a very complex exercise. While speaking to me, a feminine voice suddenly said in the middle of a DRV communication, obviously speaking to another person in her world 'Você que sabe tem de falar!' (You who know must speak!).

Can Animals Communicate?

Another thrilling event happened in 1999 when one evening a faint voice came from the loudspeaker of one of the radios and said 'É a Nisha, nós estamos aqui!' (It is Nisha. We are here!). Nisha was one of my beautiful beloved Doberman dogs, the mother of a numerous family of which four puppies stayed and lived with their parents in my house until, to my terrible distress, the hour arrived when, one by one, they all had to leave this world. I was filled with awe and emotion when I heard through DRV that little, feminine, childlike voice say 'Nisha', and the next day I asked the communicators if it had really been my Nisha who had spoken the day before. To my amazement their clear reply (readers can listen to it on the CD) was, 'Sim, por acaso; foi p'ra ti!' (Yes, it happens that it was; it was for you!). On another occasion, one of the masculine direct radio voices said to me, 'We are in contact with Nisha and she wants to speak with you.' I then asked, 'Do animals in your world have the autonomy to say they want to speak with somebody [in this case with me]?' And one of the communicators replied, 'It is more or less so.' (A sample of the little voices which on different occasions identified themselves as belonging to Nisha is included in the CD.)

I spoke about Lady before. She was one of my most cherished Doberman puppies and the last one to leave this world. She was delicate, nervous, sensitive, and seemed able to see the 'Unseen'. She used to sit for long periods watching a corner of the room, slowly moving her head from side to side as if following a very interesting scene, not paying attention to anything else around her. Or she would stand in the garden following something that was happening in the sky that nobody else and none of the other dogs could see, for as long as 20 minutes without moving from the spot. She died here in Galicia when she was ten years old on March 30, 1999, after a few years of suffering from a difficult heart condition. On one of the tapes, I found a little voice pronouncing 'Lady' very delicately some time after her death, obviously recorded through the EVP method.

The gratitude I feel for these moving, delicate contacts (there have been others since then) is beyond words. They convey to me the vision of a superior world much fairer than our own. A holistic world where, as Rio do Tempo have put it, 'All beings are equal.' A world all encompassing and all understanding. A world where shape is much less important than in our world. A world that, therefore, is 'closer to the truth', as communicators from Rio do Tempo have told me.

A Protocol of Verification

At the beginning of the year 1999, when my DRV contacts had attained an impressive level both in number and quality of communications, I became very worried by the fact that I was not doing much about the whole issue. I rightly thought that if somebody receives information which, as it seemed, comes from another level of existence, the person concerned should unfailingly disseminate it and share it with others.

In Spain or Portugal there is not much preoccupation about or interest in the hypothesis of survival of physical death. There is, of course, Sinesio Darnell (a pioneer in the field of electronic communication), who lives in Barcelona, and I had spoken with him about my ITC contacts. Sinesio is a nice man and became a good friend. He was interested but I needed someone to advise me on what to do to accomplish what I thought was my responsibility. For over a year, Carlos Fernández, the extremely serious and honest man who has accompanied me in this path from the very beginning and who has stayed on it until today, and I had explored all possible, imaginable hypotheses to determine that the phenomena we were experiencing were normal instead of anomalous, but to no avail. We always came back to the conclusion that the voices were what they seemed to be – communications from another level of existence. I should explain here that Carlos is a very good friend, a rational person, more inclined to be skeptical than gullible, and our relationship has always been purely of friendship, comradeship and shared interests.

I tried by all means to find a knowledgeable person who would be willing to help me in the task of spreading my results internationally, something that had become a major priority for me. As I explained before, by upbringing, education and profession I was a person with no connections in or understanding of the world of anomalous experiences or of the parapsychological community, something which I did not even know existed.

When I started my ITC experiences, I became a member of the British SPR in an attempt to comprehend what was happening. My proficiency in English allowed me to contact one of the names I saw in the *Journal* of the SPR, namely Professor David Fontana, a former President of the Society and currently a Life Vice President and Chair of the Society's Survival Research Committee. I wrote to him and told him what I had been experiencing in my house, and that Rio do Tempo (Timestream) was the identification I had received from the communicators. I also gave him details of some of the communications I had received. He was familiar with the title, Timestream, from accounts of the well-publicized Luxembourg phenomena, and he informed me that he was very interested in following the case. I immediately invited him to visit me in order to witness and, if possible, to participate in some of my DRV experiments, but due to other commitments he was unable to take up this invitation immediately. However, I was able to meet him in Britain and we took the opportunity to exchange more information. I was very happy with this connection because I realized he would be able to advise me on what to do. And so, through an extensive correspondence, I kept him informed in detail about what was occurring.

In the year 2001, he was finally able to visit me at my

residence in Lyon where I was then stationed as Consul-General of Portugal. This was a period when the communicators were speaking with great frequency, practically day and night, naturally in Portuguese, often carrying on with their own research in the form of the many repetitions of strings of words that I have mentioned on several occasions elsewhere in this book. Professor Fontana visited me in July, and on the evening of the 16th the communicators were speaking more or less understandably in Portuguese, apparently among themselves, now and then addressing a few words to me. Suddenly David Fontana, who was in the studio with me, without giving me previous warning or information, addressed the communicators and asked them to repeat 'Hello David'.

An attempt appeared to be made at this repetition, but we were unable to detect if it was correct or not. There was a lot of 'white noise' in the studio because, as usual, five radios were connected simultaneously and the sound of the voices echoed inside the rather small room. Furthermore, the voices sounded as they often do, i.e., as if they came from inside a funnel. It was difficult to understand much of what they were trying to say beyond such things as 'É a voz do Tempo' (It is the voice of Tempo [Rio do Tempo] or '...a gente fala do Tempo' (We speak from Tempo [Rio do Tempo]), 'somos mortos' (we are dead), 'é o Rio do Tempo' (It is Rio do Tempo) and occasional replies to my questions. Nevertheless, the next day I transferred the recording of the evening before to my computer and listened to the voices carefully with the help of Sound Forge. Some ten seconds after David asked for the repetition, one of the voices that was constantly speaking to other voices could be heard saying nonchalantly 'Alô, alô' (notice the use of 'Hello' in Portuguese). And suddenly there it was. Thirty seconds after David's request, a very different voice from the other voices, which seemed to be speaking among themselves, said softly with perfect pronunciation, 'Hello David.' This was a masculine voice of beautiful timbre that spoke the words with great tranquility at completely normal speed. To the ear, this sounded as natural as a normal male voice uttering skillfully and surely, 'Hello David,'. To this day I could not guarantee that this was a DRV. It sounds like a well-structured, perfectly articulated DRV without any distortion. But there is a slight possibility that it could have been an EVP, which would explain the fact that we did not hear it when it was pronounced. On the other hand, it could very well have been a DRV that we did not hear because of the heavy interference of the other voices and the excitement always brought about by the interaction with the communicators. It was also on this occasion, when David Fontana was trying to talk with the communicators through DRV, that a masculine voice suddenly yelled, (immediately after he addressed the communicators with 'Rio do Tempo...') 'Help me prove I'm alive!' Naturally, we were absolutely thrilled and when David had to leave we agreed that he would come back to witness other DRV communications.

This is what happened in Vigo during a holiday period in Galicia: It was the late afternoon of a beautifully clear and warm autumn day, October 2. The voices were again speaking loudly in the studio because, as usual, at their request, the radios were on 'for their work.' David and I went upstairs to the studio to listen and try to speak with them. The voices were saying 'somos do outro mundo' (We are from the other world), 'somos mortos', 'somos Rio do Tempo', and so on, mixed with uninterrupted speech to each other that could not be directly understood.

Again suddenly, without previous warning of any kind to me, David said, 'Rio do Tempo, can you say 'How are you?'' I have to confess that I became petrified when I heard him asking for this. In a second, one thousand thoughts crossed my head – what if they could not repeat 'How are you?' If that were the case what would David think? Would he doubt my honesty and perhaps imagine that I had an accomplice hidden somewhere outside or in the garden who was radio receiving/transmitting for me? This would certainly be a purposeless, bizarre idea to put forward but I got really worried because ITC contacts are a delicate issue that is not controlled by the experimenter, and I did not know David well enough to identify what might be in his mind. David asked one time; we did not hear any clear reply (and my heart sank), although we could certainly hear voices that appeared to be speaking to us. He then asked again and this time, just a couple of seconds after his request, a loud, clear, perfectly formed masculine voice replied back, 'How are you?' We both clearly heard this magnificent 'How are you?' instantly and I was overwhelmed with joy. I can be heard in the recording screaming with delight immediately after the communicators repeated 'How are you?', as David had requested. We almost jumped with the excitement (I certainly did!), and I can be heard in the recording clapping my hands and thanking the communicators with great enthusiasm (See CD).

At a certain point in this DRV dialogue, after the requested repetition, one of the communicators said clearly, obviously to David: 'Eu confio (Portuguese; 'I trust' in English), do you know what is true to you?' The observation could not have been more pertinent! We stayed for some time in the studio speaking to the communicators. And after David addressed them with, 'It is wonderful to speak to you!' one of them responded with 'So, how are you?' in a friendly, amused tone. Another communicator remarked in French, also apparently to David: 'Bonjour!' 'Rio do Tempo' could be heard several times. This was indeed a glorious confirmation of the reality and autonomy of the communicators and I rejoiced.

When we listened to the long recording of that afternoon, with the computer and the help of Sound Forge software, it became obvious that the communicators had already repeated the sentence the first time David asked them to. Their first repetition happened also two seconds after David's request. However, there was a lot of 'white noise' because, as usual, the five radios were connected simultaneously, and we missed their first repetition, but readers can listen to it on the CD. The first voice was a little lower in amplitude but also clear. During this same DRV contact, a very loud EVP saying, 'Há marcado ruído' (There is a lot of noise) was registered on the tape as well.

But David Fontana's story was to continue! This time in Lyon, on the 27th of November of the same year, David again came to my house and on the evening of his arrival when he entered the small studio where the radios were on for their work, it was the turn of the communicators to immediately salute him with 'How are you?' even before he could say anything. We both heard and understood perfectly their welcoming words and reacted with explosions of great pleasure that were registered on the tape. What a thrilling event to be greeted by communicators from another world with the same phrase that one of the two partici-pants in this remarkable event had addressed them, and had requested them to repeat almost two months before in another country and another studio! This whole story is a formidable demonstration of the reality and autonomy of the communi-cators, and for me it is an unforgettable and very moving occasion. One could not ask for very much more.

Chapter 6

Content of the Communications

Transformation in the Experimenter

The amazing events of the year 1998 changed my whole life. I would wake up in the morning in a state of joy, anticipating the end of the day when my invisible friends would perhaps speak to me again and answer my questions about some of the existential issues that have interested me ever since I can remember. I used to ask them all kinds of questions, from philosophical ones on the meaning and purpose of life, to more trivial ones such as the living conditions of my beloved deceased family members and my pets in their new world, and many others on the nature of their world.

It is extremely difficult to properly describe the fascination I felt for those voices when, night after night, they answered my questions. The communicators' comments and replies were usually simple and very logical but, although this is perhaps difficult for readers to understand and for me to explain, they were logical from a radically different perspective to that of the usual human point of view. Their opinions and explanations resonated in the very core of my Self, as if the communicators and I were two glasses made of the same crystal. I remember that tears often came to my eyes whenever I thought about the extraordinary things they had told me in the course of some very especial communications. In some strange way, it was as if I had always known that life was as they described it but my mind had not allowed the information to surface and become part of my normal thinking until then. I suppose that this involuntary rejection is caused by what I call mental patterning, the acquired models that become part of us and do not allow us to be free, even when we believe that, as in my case, we are open, rebellious and unconventional.

The conflicting reaction I experienced was caused, from one side, by the incredulity of someone who was educated under very rational and conventional principles, even though I spontaneously disagreed with the majority of them from an early age, and the awe induced by the communications and their content, from the other side. I used to think, 'So it is true – there is another world and its laws and ways are very different from ours!' and I could not get over it. 'There is another world, there is another way,' as the communicators put it and in that world, life is more just and purer than in our poor planet, so devastated by human greed and insensitivity! My whole being was inflamed with the joy of this discovery which meant a very great deal to me and suddenly made life worthwhile. Thus savoring with delight the magnificent opportunity so unexpectedly offered to me, I asked Rio do Tempo hundreds of questions during their long periods of contact.

Recalling the many questions that I untiringly put to the communicators brings to mind a wonderfully clear DRV, received by the Portuguese experimenter Luísa Alcântara during her own ITC experimentation, which I listened to. When she once asked the communicating entity, 'Can you hear me?' a loud, clear feminine voice said almost immediately, 'Deve você fazer uma pergunta, mas com tantas perguntas fico morto!' (It is up to you to ask a question, but with so many questions I will continue to be dead!) This remark is particularly interesting for several reasons – it shows a wonderful sense of humor (a characteristic of many ITC voices) for it not only tells Luísa that she is the one who should ask a question, a clear reference to the practice generally followed by ITC experimenters. But it also expresses the very human feeling of somebody who is tired of being bombarded with never-ending questions, which, no matter the identity of the researcher, in many instances must be identical. A similar incident happened at the beginning of my DRV contacts. The communicators had instructed me to, 'Speak directly,' and a masculine voice started one of the next contacts after this advice with, 'Pergunte, pergunte!' (Ask, ask!), even before I could say anything.

I am often asked which message I consider the most important one among the many communications that I have received from Rio do Tempo Station, and I usually respond with: Survival of physical death is the Natural Law. Survival is part of the Natural Law and no life form can escape from it. This concept has been expressed frequently in Rio do Tempo's communications and is implied in many others. When I once asked Carlos de Almeida what happens to plants when they die, he replied: 'Não se esqueça que as plantas são seres do vosso mundo, do outro mundo passam sempre todos para este'. (Do not forget that plants are beings of your world, all from the other world always pass into this world [theirs]). An entity replied to the same question, put by Hans Otto König to his own communicators, with, 'All life continues.' While at Marcello Bacci's Center in Grosseto, the communicators affirmed in my presence, '... In questo universo niente perisce, cambia semplicemente forma; la legge della natura che governa questo regno perverrà a la conoscenza del tutto.' (Translation from the Italian original: In this universe nothing perishes, it simply changes shape; the Law of Nature that governs this realm will reach the understanding of the whole) (Cardoso, 2005).

Purpose of the Communications

A lot could be said about this subject. Besides the obvious purpose of informing us that life does not finish with physical death, one of the main goals of the most comprehensive ITC communications appears to be an attempt to contribute to the expansion of human consciousness, by conveying to us information of high ethical content which breaks with conventional human values. The Technician said in Luxembourg, 'ITC is the most important instrument to make human consciousness get out of its state of sleepiness. To achieve this goal we need bridges and builders between your world and the world of the spirit...' (Schäfer 1993, pp. 113-114). It is also reported that the deceased Konstantin Raudive spoke about the importance of consciousness development during a post-mortem telephone conversation with a French lady, Aline Piget, in 1997. During this remarkable event, the first one of its kind in France, Raudive said: 'I would like you to know, dear Aline, that the object of an earthly life is not just the goodness. The object is to be conscious...' (Théry, 2000).

From the beginning of the reception of anomalous voices on Earth, to Maggy and Jules Harsch-Fischbach, Adolf Homes and others, the communicators have reiterated that humans should critically examine their values and their ways of thinking. Let me quote here just one such example: To Hans Otto König communicators from Group Centrale said in 1988, in addition to other equally 'revolutionary' statements, 'If you believe that man is the crown of creation, this is wrong. A plant or an animal can be higher developed [spiritually]' (Senkowski, König, personal correspondence, 2008). And on another occasion, also to Hans Otto König, 'There are no religions [in their world]; you have invented your own religions' (Schäfer ibid, 1993). In Luxembourg the Technician confirmed this statement with similar words and added that only the prayer that comes from the heart is worthwhile and we should understand that prayer is also '...to smile to a child, caress a dog, rejoice in the color of a flower.' What could be truer, more beautiful and more unusual for us modern-times humans?

Important clues on the subject of consciousness development were also given by the people from Rio do Tempo Station. On December 6, 1998, they said, 'Falamos p'ro mundo inteiro, a abertura de um caminho p'ra lá do tempo' (We speak to the whole world, the opening of a path beyond time). This I inter-preted as them telling us that their contacts are designed to contribute to the opening [in our consciousness] of a path beyond time [our world and its values]. On a different occasion (July 28, 2000), a voice replied to my usual question of, 'Who is speaking?' with 'Nós falamos do outro mundo, os humanos precisam de saber da luz' (We speak from the other world, humans need to know about the light). (See CD).

There are many examples of ground-breaking information among the most advanced ITC communications. It all prompts us to acknowledge the falseness of prevailing human concepts and anthropomorphic views and attitudes.

Some Highly Significant Messages on the Purpose of the Communications

A piece of utmost importance was transmitted to the Luxembourg group in the presence of eight people (B.W., Jean-Paul Seyler, George Meek, Andreas Resch, Ernst and Adelheid Senkowski, Maggy and Jules Harsch-Fischbach). From Professor Senkowski's book and with his permission, I quote the following extract about the extraordinary episode:

Henry Sainte-Claire Deville made contact on May 2, 1987, at 8 pm, as the speaker of the transgroup *LIFELINE* (other world partner of American Metascience). He spoke in English with a conspicuous French accent, directly via the loudspeaker of an Ultra-Short Wave receiver of the ESB (Euro Signal Bridge, one of the Luxembourg bridges of contact) within the 90 MHz range; the intelligibility of his speech was 100 %. Investigations showed that the 'drop-in' communicator *DEVILLE*, unknown to all those present, had been a remarkable 19th century French chemist who, amongst others, was the first to study the properties of crystalline silicon. The year 1881 that he mentioned as that of his passing is correct.

This is what he said: *My name is Henry Sainte Claire Deville. I left your world in 1881, and I am speaking to you in my name and in the name of our staff from LIFELINE, the scientists. Your project, as well as those from LIFELINE and from TIMESTREAM, is to set fire to minds, to set fire to minds in your world, and in that moment to try to master time. I can give you a few explanations.*

The void dreams the universe, but the void is unconscious. Universe has consciousness and it can control the voice. A strong force, the inertia of normality, reigns in the universe. So the universe always chooses the same state as before, it sustains itself, it limits itself. I repeat: the universe is dreamt by the void. It is varied out of grains, grains of virtual existence, grains called selectons. Selectons are really tiny dots consisting of a circle rolled up compactly. Forever they roll back into the void, forever other bits of void roll back to replace them exactly. All these selectons are rolled up compactly in the same direction, thus time flows in one direction in the universe. In our space selectons are not rolled up, so there in the Never-Ever all time is one and timeless. (Senkowski, 1995).

The need to 'set fire to minds, to set fire to minds in (our) world' is clearly pointed out as the principal goal of all those involved in Instrumental Transcommunication projects between the two dimensions. But as early as Raudive's time, a similar expression had already been used by the invisible communicators. It is included in the tape appended to the English version of Konstantin Raudive's most famous work, *Breakthrough*. The investigator asked the communicators if research into the voice phenomenon had any significance and a Latvian voice replied, 'You are burning people!' I have a copy of Raudive's original tape, which was a very special gift from my dear friend Hernani Guimarães Andrade, and I have personally listened to that very clear voice. The remarkable analogy with the Luxembourg DRV needs no further comment.

On February 8, 1987, in Luxembourg, the deceased

Konstantin Raudive speaking to Prof. Senkowski reiterated that theme:

> Dear colleague Senkowski. You know, natural science is skeptical; of course also the majority of men in the street. Nowadays all, from infancy onwards, have been educated in a materialistic life view. So this is natural: new ideas are only adopted by the majority of people if they recognize them (as) suiting their own worldview. **Our task should be to widen such a worldview** [state of consciousness] **and endeavor to create a new one in which many truths will have a place.** (Message conveyed through the ESB; Senkowski ibid, 1989, pp 270-271).

Still on another occasion, while Adolf Homes was in hospital, on June 28, 1995, a computer-printout from Transgroup 2109 was produced by the system at his house that said:

> Hier 2109 für Herrn Dr. Senkowski. Beschäftigung mit Metaphysik wichtig. Die Edukation des Menschseins im geistig kosmischen Sinne bleibt unserer aller Aufgabe. (Translation: Here 2109 for Dr. Senkowski. Engagement in metaphysics important. **The education of human beings in the spiritual cosmic sense remains a task for all of us).** (Senkowski, 2008; personal correspondence.)

I have already mentioned in the Introduction, Carlos de Almeida's sudden and unexpected statement, apparently referring to ITC contacts, 'É p'ra essa gente humilde, é convocar o amor, panaceia do mundo, seria bonito, não é?'(Literal translation: It is for humble people, it is to call upon love, panacea of the world. It would be beautiful, would it not?). This simple message is at the core of another great purpose of ITC – to tell everybody that they can reach out to the next world and that through love the world can be healed.

In April 2007, Marcello Bacci's communicators repeated nearly the same in Grosseto, to Father François Brune, during a DRV session in which the renowned philosopher Ervin Laszlo also participated:

.... Father what you do is very beautiful, you must start again. The instruments, which are wonderful instruments in themselves, can change the hearts (apparently referring to the communications). It is fair to have these things into account, it is good that the priests use them appropriately, they prompt an impulse for the return, and that ... (unintelligible) ... upon people. (*Le Messager* 2008, 64, pp. 14-16).

A Communicator Called Carlos de Almeida

I think that the amazing adventure of my ITC results was made possible by Carlos de Almeida. About him, said an EVP voice unexpectedly recorded during one of my first contacts, 'Amou a gente, muita gente' (He loved people, many people.) (Included in the CD.)

After that unbelievable evening of March 11, 1998, he spoke with me almost everyday for over one year – always the same powerful masculine voice with its distinctive timbre and expressions. He used to joke with me, to speak with me about my beloved deceased Doberman dogs and comfort me for their absence, to scold me, to playfully invite me 'to dance the waltz' and so on. He was patient with my questions and complaints but he was also strong and sure of what he was teaching me, never indulging me but also never reproaching me for anything.

One of Carlos de Almeida's particularly interesting messages contained the following statement, amongst others '...Já estou livre de ilusão...'. (Literal translation: I am already free from illusion). It is interesting to compare this statement with one made by Myers in *The Road to Immortality*. Myers refers to the so-called Third Plane in the afterlife (the Plane above Hades which exists just above the physical world) as the '...illusion-land in which you wear an etheric body. It is of a finer or more tenuous matter than the physical form...'. On another occasion in the same chapter, when speaking of the Fourth Plane or the Plane of Colour, he tells us that it is

the state beyond Illusion, when you are living consciously and are sensible of your subtle body, you dwell in a world which is the original of the earth. Briefly, the earth is an ugly smudged copy of the world wherein dwells the subtle soul in its subtle body...

This would seem to suggest that by moving beyond illusion, Carlos de Almeida was on the point of progressing to the Fourth Plane.

Carlos de Almeida seemed to be an experienced and very knowledgeable communicator. In fact, since he announced that he was about to leave Rio do Tempo's world (presumably by moving up to the Fourth Plane) the communications from the station have suffered greatly in quality and in regularity. He had become such a customary presence in my house that I took it for granted that he would always be there and welcomed him almost every night as a wonderful and very special friend. But one evening when, as usual, I asked him, 'How are you Carlos de Almeida?' he replied, 'Prestes a partir' ([I'm] about to leave) and a few months later other voices informed me that he was no longer in Rio do Tempo's world; he had moved on into a world '[that was] like a sun,' a world from where he could not speak to our world.

It was extremely bizarre to hear an interlocutor from another world reply to me, 'o Carlos de Almeida está no sol!' (Carlos de Almeida is in the sun) when I enquired about him. And when I, struck by the oddness of it all, requested them to confirm if he was in a sun, they said, 'Não é o teu sol, mas é um Sol.' (It is not your sun but it is a sun). It seems pertinent to make a connection here to another sentence contained in one of his conversations. He said speaking of his world, 'Isto aqui tem muito serviço, é o portão da luz, é bonito aqui'. (There is a lot of work here. It is the gate to the light. It is beautiful here'. Thus, if Carlos de Almeida's former world was 'the gate to the light', it seems coherent to say that the world he moved to is 'like a sun'. After his departure life was never again the same for me.

Most of the information from Rio do Tempo Station that I will pass on to you in this chapter was conveyed to me by Carlos de Almeida.

On the Subject of Death

The subject of death is undoubtedly an issue of paramount importance for humankind although apparently not for other species. However, the majority of people when questioned about it will say that they 'don't care about death', while many will say that they 'are not interested in discussing the subject', and still others will say that they 'do not mind dying', etc. Only very few will confess the truth and say that they are 'terrified by death'. I think that fear is at the bottom of the former rather usual statements; an intense fear that prevents modern humans from facing the issue of death. It was different in older times that we consider dark, but which were perhaps more enlightened from the point of view of spiritual (non-material) matters.

This modern fear of death is so strong that it can even prevent people from recognizing that death exists and it certainly makes them live as if it did not. I think that the utterly materialistic attitude of our time is greatly responsible for this situation. We are conditioned, and mental patterning again plays a determinant role in this approach, to think of things that we cannot see as non-existent. Indeed, we have reached a point where anything that cannot be seen, heard, touched, smelled or tasted either does not exist or does not matter. In my opinion nothing could be less intelligent or more brutal in terms of sensitivity. Behind this attitude lies the misunderstood concept of rationalism that became the philosophical foundation of capitalism and consumerism.

A common feature of ITC communications since Jürgenson and Raudive is that, according to the communicators, the great majority of them originate from the deceased. Friedrich Jürgenson was not experimenting for anomalous voices, and although he was a man interested in spiritual matters, he had no idea that such a thing (to record voices claiming to come from the deceased) could happen to him or even that it could happen at all. But his voices claimed to belong to the deceased from the very beginning. Even Jürgenson, albeit a man of great sensitivity and intelligence, refused to accept the idea, and for some time he thought that the voices originated in extraterrestrial intelligence. However, as he explains in his books, with the pursuing of the communications he was forced to discard that idea. Konstantin Raudive also received many messages on the subject of death which confirmed that the communicators were deceased people (*Breakthrough*, 1971, pp. 147-152).

My communicators tell us that the time of death is predetermined. 'Anabela o tempo está marcado, pode dar o passo e o compromisso, está marcado para toda a gente!' (Anabela, the time is predetermined. You can 'make the step and the commitment'. It is predetermined for everybody [and every being as they confirmed later]). And Hans Otto König's communicators used practically the same words 'The time of death is predetermined for each life' (Schäfer, 1993, Portuguese ed. p.100). However, when, after listening to the above statement I asked Rio do Tempo if chance existed, they said, 'Há o acaso sim.' (Yes, chance does exist). This statement drives me to consider that perhaps only the most important events of each life are predetermined in a kind of compromise between the deterministic view of some Spiritualists and the random chance view of some materialists.

In an extremely interesting anticipation of inevitable events, the communicators, apparently speaking among themselves, referred to my own death in these terms: 'Anabela já está morta, já está morta já está feliz!' (Literal translation: Anabela is already dead. She is already dead. She is already happy!) Will this phrase be related to the fact that they 'live outside of time', as they affirm? It is very likely that it is, but maybe it also reflects my attitude toward death after I started to get positive results in ITC experimentation. In my most optimistic days I think of my own death as liberation and a wonderful adventure that will reunite me with my deceased loved ones in a splendid new world. But sometimes I also have doubts about the whole process, although I am firmly convinced that they are the unfortunate consequence of our deeply rooted materialistic education and values, which are extremely difficult to wipe out because they have become an intrinsic part of our mental universe. Another glorious statement from our invisible friends says, 'Rio do Tempo, a morte é tão bonita! É feia é no espaço.' (Rio do Tempo, death is so beautiful! It is only ugly in space [our space-time].)

I will share with my readers a touching little story that explores the death process a little further. I had asked my communicators to help me find a little dog, Rita, that had disappeared from the shelter that I have made for abandoned animals, and to this request they replied, 'A Rita está no nosso mundo.' (Rita is in our world). When a couple of days later I asked how she was, to my surprise they said: 'A Rita está no silencio!' (Rita is in the silence!) She was found dead near my property in Portugal that houses the dogs' sanctuary a short time after all this had happened. I continued to question the communicators on the meaning of their expression, 'Rita is in the silence,' and they then told me that it was a stage comparable to a very deep meditation. In his turn, says Myers through Geraldine Cummins' automatic writing: 'Between each plane there is this lapse into apparent oblivion, a stilling of all processes, a great calm.' (Cummins, 1932, p. 67). What a stunning analogy!

On the Subject of Suffering

According to my communicators, suffering is very important for everybody. Most of us wonder why some people (or animals) have to face so much suffering during their lifetime, while for others things seem to be a lot easier. Many of us also wonder about the deep meaning of suffering. It was with these thoughts in my mind that I once asked Rio do Tempo what the meaning of suffering was. Their reply was simple. 'It has all, it has all the meaning.' And when I asked them to comment on this, they said that 'it is very important for the spiritual progress [of the beings who endure it].' The explanation given by the Technician in Luxembourg about the suffering of mankind is even more enlightening. Said the high entity:

> The pain and suffering that each person has to bear is part of his own self, partially caused by his own actions or designed by a high power. In both cases it serves to stimulate understanding, improvement and perfection (e. g. Locher and Harsch, French ed., 1989).

Reincarnation

The existence or otherwise of reincarnation seemed to be a very difficult issue to get replies to. I finally got one faint voice, so faint that I cannot guarantee its correct interpretation beyond any doubt, which seems to say, 'Only [reincarnation] when there is no other way [for progression].'

In Luxembourg, the Technician confirmed the existence of reincarnation and said about it:

> You may not like it but it is as I have told you: Reincarnation

exists. There are parallel worlds! The beings evolve in the incompressible wheel of life. Some have arrived at a point of development that allows them a better understanding. Reincarnation means progression forward not backward. Animals too are subject to the cycle of reincarnation. Man does not reincarnate in an animal body. Important Earth personalities can be born again as simple people if they used their previous life only to impose their power upon others. Illnesses and infirmities have a purpose. Do not judge the fate of other people. If we deem it important to inform you of the reasons why some people are particularly tested we will do so. Some individuals need help and advice while others reject any help as you yourself have already found out. Those people have chosen a life full of adversity even before their reincarnation.' (Locher and Harsch, 1995, French ed.)

Spiritual Development and Ethical Values in the Next Dimension of Life

Several experimenters report receiving elevated ethical teachings from their 'transpartners', but I have to admit that in general I have not received such comments spontaneously. Nonetheless, I must also say that Rio do Tempo's teachings are highly ethical, although they were never imposed on me; on the whole, they came in response to my queries. One exception to this was a spontaneous, very strange sounding masculine voice that repeated loudly several times, 'Falem de amor, têm tempo.' (Speak of love, you have time.) The very deep voice articulated the words very, very slowly as if dragging the syllables with great effort. I remember that when I first listened to this raucous Direct Radio Voice, a voice I had never heard before, nor heard again afterwards, I felt apprehensive and even scared, but as soon as I understood the content any apprehension disappeared.

As I have stated before, I am neither a Spiritualist nor a Spiritist. As a matter of fact, I do not follow, neither do I believe in, any religious practice but, from the information contained in ITC messages, we can easily assume that the purpose of existence is to experience life and through it to learn and grow. When I asked my communicators what was the fundamental condition for spiritual progression, they said something that initially puzzled me: 'É o tempo e é o espaço.' (It is time and it is space.) I pondered on this statement and concluded that it applied to life on Earth, therefore in time and space. Continuing in the same vein, I then asked if life should be preserved by all possible means and they replied positively to this query. It is important to emphasize that when I refer to 'life' it is implicit that I mean all life, no matter in which form – animal, vegetable or mineral. Naturally, the concept of spiritual development is intimately connected to, and could be exchanged for, the concept of expansion of consciousness that the communicators use in a cosmic sense, as expressed in the above quotation.

I love animals and I am very interested and concerned with their fate. I feel very strongly about them because animals possess a wonderful natural innocence, a genuineness, which I intuitively perceive as coming directly from the divine, i.e. the essence of life, and in general they live under the ruthless power of humans. I used to question the communicators on the living conditions of animals in their world and also on the life of plants. I asked, for instance, if plants also felt suffering, something that intrigues and disturbs me, and inquired about their consciousness. To these questions they replied, 'All beings in the world have consciousness,' and 'All beings in the world feel suffering.' One day, when my question was how animals progressed [in our world], an interesting response came forward, 'Through the hardships of the Natural Law.'

Continuing on the same line of what I said at the beginning of the chapter, I repeat that the information conveyed by the communicators has always fascinated me for its intrinsic logic – albeit in disagreement to what we normally consider common sense – one which, at the core of my being, I perceive as the deep truth that lies beneath appearances. For instance, when I asked what the main goal of animals in their world was, they replied through DRV: 'Também tentam saber mais.' (They also try to know more.) Indeed, I think it is only natural that the Cosmos in its supreme wisdom makes no distinctions between the apparently different life forms which form an intrinsic, deeply interrelated constituent part of the same domain of reality, i.e., life on Earth. Certainly the Cosmos is not anthropomorphic or anthropocentric! The high entity that we call the Technician put it clearly when he emphasized that respect towards every life form is part of the spiritual progress of men. He also recommended that in the future, ITC should be associated with human rights and the protection of animals and nature. On another occasion, he said: 'The occupants of the Earth have to learn to think differently. With the help of ITC some will learn the worthlessness of their material thinking and will turn toward spiritual interests.' (Locher and Harsch ibid, 1989).

The equality of all life seems to be a basic pillar of the next world's ethical structure. Among similar statements, Rio do Tempo once said, 'Aqui no Rio do Tempo somos todos iguais.' (Here in Rio do Tempo we are all equal.) While Swejen Salter declared in Luxembourg '…in case people on your Earth think that we worry too much about the animals, it would be good if they understand that in our sphere one life has the same value as another one' (Schäfer ibid, 1993, p. 202). Hans Otto König's 'transpartners' used almost identical words: 'Here we are all equal,' while specifically addressing the issue of values with, 'Remember that we have a world just like yours but with different material values' (Schäfer, 1993, p. 100). On the same topic, one of Konstantin Raudive's voice contacts declared, 'Kant does not have any importance here,' (Raudive ibid, p. 30). Rio do Tempo communicators prosaically say, 'Este mundo é o do 'elme' [alma] que aposta noutro lado.' (Literal translation: This is the world of the soul that bets [takes a chance] somewhere else.) For obvious reasons I like to keep the translations of the communications as literal as possible; however, in this case I will add that my interpretation of their statement is that their world has different values.

Notice the odd semantics of the sentence and the corruption of the word 'alma' (*'elme'*). Language corruption can be found in some ITC audio communications. Another relevant example of this linguistic event can be found in the phrase that Carlos de Almeida once used to confirm that he was speaking from Rio do Tempo Station. I had asked if it were him speaking from Rio do Tempo Station and his reply literally said: 'Sim, o prometiu!' (Yes, as promised!) However, the correct form of the verb is 'prometido' not *'prometiu'*, a word which does not exist in the Portuguese language.

Perhaps one of the most clarifying examples of the next world's main values was conveyed by Rio do Tempo communicators through the transpicture of a mask. As mentioned in previous chapters I started experimenting, together with our little group, in video images. One of the very interesting images we received was of a beautiful mask that one day appeared recorded on the video tape while I experimented with the Schreiber method. It fitted into the content of a conversation that I had had with Carlos de Almeida through DRV a few days before.

Due to the volume of contacts received, we had decided to stop the experimentation with images to work with the voices only. But I very much wanted to resume that particular practice, and on October 12, 1998 asked Carlos de Almeida if we could ever hope to obtain clear transimages from his world. His loud and comprehensible reply, which readers can listen to on the CD, said, 'Conforme, execute uma máscara de escultor, sabe qual é?' (It depends. Execute a sculptor's mask. Do you know what that is?) Indeed, I didn't know 'what that was' and took almost one year to find out. It was only when I met an aged, famous Portuguese sculptor during the inauguration of one of his sculptures in a public square in La Coruña, where I was accredited as Consul General of Portugal, that I asked him what it meant and he explained to me that a sculptor's mask was the name normally given to the wax mould that is taken of a deceased person's face to make a post-mortem sculpture.

A couple of days after Carlos de Almeida replied to my question on the images, while I experimented with the video camera and the Schreiber method, the beautiful, elusive face of a woman half-covered by a sliding mask appeared recorded on the video tape. I thought that the coincidence between the conversation with Carlos de Almeida and the lovely image of a mask was remarkable but I was not fully satisfied, and sometime later asked Rio do Tempo what the deep meaning of the mask was. I think that the symbolic image together with their straightforward but profound reply represent a wonderful example of what their world stands for. 'A máscara é a maneira de nós te dizermos que o nosso mundo descobre a verdade.' (The mask is our way to tell you that our world unveils the truth.)

Location, Descriptions of the Next World, and the Communicators' Presence in the Experimenter's Place.

It is extremely difficult to get information from our friends on some specific issues, such as the location and the characteristics of the next world. It may seem naïve but there was a time when I used to insist on the question: 'Rio do Tempo, where is your world?' without getting any responses. However, one evening, when I once again asked the same question, a loud, authoritarian voice suddenly interrupted to say, 'A isso *non!*' (Not to that! [No reply to that question].)

Proper descriptions of their world are also not easily obtained. Besides 'A world very similar to yours', or 'It is good' and Carlos de Almeida's '... It is the gate to the light. It is beautiful here', I did not receive much more information about the characteristics of their world. Thus, it was very interesting for me to discover, in Raudive's *Breakthrough* (p. 152), only a short time ago, that the voices had justified the vagueness of their statements about these issues by explaining that, 'We are not allowed to tell,' 'Konstantin, it is not quite like that,' and, 'We cannot report more precisely.' As I mentioned before, my communicators did not reply to some of my questions and one day a strong voice even interrupted to say with great authority, 'Não responda à pergunta.' (Do not answer the question.)

Notwithstanding what I just said, a reference to 'above' in regard to the location of their world is quite frequent. In the course of the research projects, sponsored by two anonymous international institutions which I was entrusted to develop, a very interesting remark that literally says this was recorded on July 28, 2008. During strictly controlled experiments carried out in the Laboratory of Acoustics at the Department of Telecommunications of Vigo University, a feminine voice appeared recorded in the University's digital recorder, which said, 'Estamos aqui por cima!', while a juvenile voice added, 'Só isso!' (We are here above / only that!)

'Só' was also the name of a dog that I had found many years ago in the most atrocious conditions and had rescued and sheltered until he left this world. Then one day, some years ago, I found myself thinking about 'Só' and spoke about him with the communicators. A couple of days later, during a DRV session, immediately following a kind of odd growling noise, a voice said, 'All right Só, we'll go up in a moment.'

On another instance, during the moving conversation I had with my grandmother through DRV about her house and rosemary, after her first affirmative reply to my question if she remembered rosemary, a different feminine voice suddenly intervened to say, 'Pode seguir' (You may continue.) We proceeded with the conversation. After a couple of pauses I again addressed my grandmother with 'Grandma?' to be sure that she was still listening, and apparently the same voice as before replied, 'Ela foi já p'ra baixo.' (She already went down.) I believe that the use of the words 'above', 'go up', and 'go down' could very well be metaphors to convey to us the idea of the progressive development attained through the different stages that comprise the ladder of existence. This is a manner that we understand easily since it fits into our common concepts of higher and lower, also used by the different religions.

Another explicit example of the same image of speech was Carlos de Almeida's clear statement, when he declared in a powerful voice, '...Ele não vem e ao meu grupo desço, vou à alma!...' (...He does not come and I go down to my group. I go to the soul!...) Besides the fascinating reference to the Group Soul that I will discuss in the next chapter, his statement is also very interesting because of the expression 'I go down to my group'. Indeed, Carlos de Almeida says that he goes down to the group he belongs to and a few months later he will say that he is 'about to leave'. Everything seems to point towards the conclusion that he was almost (or already) in a higher plane from where he could come down to join his group in a lower plane. The information conveyed by Swejen Salter, the deceased scientist from another planet, to the Luxembourg's couple seems to confirm this hypothesis: 'People who share imagination and points of view join together in groups and form a unity. This unity constitutes the preliminary step for the fourth dimension' (Schäfer ibid, p. 246). And this is perhaps the explanation for the communication skills Carlos de Almeida gave proof of, in the course of the almost two years that he spoke regularly with me.

Another revealing observation made by the communicators about their world said: 'É um mundo puro, o outro mundo não é bom p'ra nós...' (It is a pure world [theirs], the other world [ours] is not good for us [them]...) (Again, most of the voices I have quoted are in the CD.)

At a later stage in my contacts, the communicators would spontaneously say surprising things such as, 'Nós estamos fora do tempo, tu estás no tempo.' (We are out of time, you are within time.) Or 'Estamos numa ponta do espaço.' (We are in an apex of space.) On another occasion, at the end of a most beautiful chant, 'Somos doutra dimensão, somos pr'a lá do tempo.' (We are from another dimension. We are from beyond time.)

The presence of the communicators in the experimenter's place has been reiterated since the very beginning of ITC contacts, even as early as Ernetti's and Gemelli's experiences. It is reported that Gemelli's father said, 'I am always with you!' (See Chapter 2), while Raudive's interlocutors used a wonderful expression, 'We never leave' (Raudive ibid, 1971). My own communicators have said innumerable times, 'Nós estamos sempre contigo.' (We are always with you.) And the same thing has happened to other operators (Schäfer ibid, 1993, Senkowski ibid, 1995). When my dog Nisha spoke through the DRV for the first time (and Carlos de Almeida confirmed the next day that indeed she had spoken) she also said, 'Nisha, nós estamos aqui!' (Nisha, we are here!) But not only do they use such typical phrases, which are common to practically every experimenter, they make use of other expressions that imply the same, such as when Rio do Tempo said, 'Vai lavar os pés.' (Go and wash your feet.) That evening I had arrived directly from the beach to go into the recording studio still carrying sand on my feet; another time they said at the beginning of the contact, 'So we have new equipment here,' (I had bought a mixing table), and so on. But when I specifically inquired if they could see our world, the replies were, 'Only some can', and on another occasion, 'It is a lot of work for us [to be able to see our world.]'

The Role of Water
As I mentioned in Chapter 4, an extraordinary sentence appeared recorded on my tape in the form of an EVP while we were

recording a DRV communication from Rio do Tempo on March 29, 1998. A beautiful and enigmatic EVP voice can be heard as loudly and clearly as a clear human voice, agreeing to a comment that my friend Carlos Fernández had made. The voice said, 'Claro que não tem nada que ver, a ilusão que temos nós, eles não me podem ouvir, tem de ser através do mar.' (Of course it has nothing to do with it [speaking loudly or lowly], the same illusion that we have. They cannot hear me. It has to be through the sea). The content of this EVP (on the CD) is very interesting for many reasons, including the fact that the communicators are able to follow closely what happens in the room, but the most puzzling one is the meaning of, 'They cannot hear me. It has to be through the sea.' What sea does the beautiful voice refer to? Is it the Atlantic Ocean that surrounds my house here in Galicia? Is it the sea of the Unconscious, or perhaps the sea of the Hermetic tradition? We really don't know. But then, what to think when the sound of water, as if somebody or something is diving or sinking, together with the sound of gurgles can be heard inter-mingled with the communicators' words in some of my DRV recordings as happens for instance in the beautiful chant that finishes with '...Somos doutra dimensão, somos p'ra lá do tempo'? (a segment of the chant is on the CD).

In addition, my curiosity was increased when I heard very similar sounds during one of Bacci's DRV sessions that I took part in, and recorded, at his Center in Grosseto. In one of her books (e.g. 1993), Hildegard Schäfer transcribes several of her own messages; on page 267 she says that one of the times when she asked the communicators if they could hear her, the voice replied, 'Here we hear sounds – a whole diving platform full of voices.' The 'sea' mentioned by Rio do Tempo's feminine voice becomes even more mysterious!

Closing Remarks

The impressive correspondence of the information received by researchers in different parts of the globe, some of whom lived in different epochs, should be sufficient to make us accept the autonomous existence of the communicators. As a matter of fact, it is not conceivable that experimenters, who do not know each other and have had no contact with each other, 'produce' with their minds, as if by an act of magic, almost identical information of a highly controversial nature that definitely shatters human mental schemes and visions of the world, including their own. To maintain this untenable hypothesis, named by some 'the psychokinetic explanation', we would have to assume that the experimenter's mind also creates other voices that order the initial anomalous ones involved in the dialogue not to reply to selected questions of a delicate nature, as I exemplified above. This appears to me to be the peak of absurdity but these days, in the world of psychical research, we can expect all kinds of abstruse arguments for still unexplainable phenomena.

Moreover, the signal containing the information conveyed by the communicators appears to be modulated from random radio noise or 'miraculously' produced on computer hard disks or monitors. And, if we take into consideration the psychokinetic hypothesis, all this would have to be accomplished without conscious intervention of the human psychokinetic agent, as if a feat of such magnitude were an easy and normal thing to do! Because his explanation is pertinent to our discussion, I will quote Friedrich Jürgenson again. When a journalist posed the following question to him: '…the possibility still exists that you, Mr. Jürgenson, are able to project this sound and voice phenomena completely unconsciously unto a tape through the power of your subconscious. Perhaps you are a kind of medium with the peculiar gift, possibly for the first time in the history of psychical research, to produce electromagnetic impulses and to send these into the ether. What would be your answer to this?'

Jürgenson replied with:

'I should feel extremely flattered by such a supposition if vanity had been my strong suit. But if we want to get to the bottom of the issue of a possible mediumistic capability on my part in a rational way, we will first have to clarify the physical origin of the voice and sound phenomena.

We know today that all sounds, whether generated by the larynx or mechanical instruments, not only produce sound waves that travel through the air but consist of electromagnetic oscillations that spread through the ether depending on their power source either as radio waves or as sound waves. Since our [EVP] phenomena cannot be sound waves – otherwise the voices would be heard by every one in the room – they must consist of electromagnetic frequencies sent into the ether by some kind of power source.

Now if we want to suppose that my subconscious represents such a power center, I would have the honor of being the biggest genius in the world capable of subconsciously producing the entire dynamics of a radio station including antenna, studio, technical personnel, musical instruments, choirs, soloists and commentators of all kind.

Besides, I would need to possess the magical gift of imitating perfectly the voices of dead people of every gender and age in the most varied languages *including voices never previously known or heard by me.*

But that is not all.

The most absurd "miracle" would consist in my ability to overpower wily nil any radio wave oscillating in the ether, namely to totally or partially alter any current radio transmission, such as the British BBC or the West German Radio Network using the "program" of my own "subconscious

113

transmitter". Not even the most powerful Russian jamming station would be capable of such an achievement.

Such a heroic act would not only exceed the achievements of good old Baron von Münchhausen but would allow me to claim godlike capabilities. A man with such capabilities would be employed right away by the secret services of the major powers with a fantastic salary and retirement benefits…'

I will make a parenthesis here to thank the Jürgenson Foundation for their kind permission to quote from the English translation of one of Friedrich Jürgenson's books (Jürgenson, 2004). As a highly intelligent, cultured and experienced researcher, Jürgenson is not only an invaluable source of information but also of enlightened pondering on the complexities of this area of study.

As mentioned above, most of the time the experimenters themselves are the first to be astounded by the content of the communications they receive. There are cases, which I prefer not to single out, when the 'revolutionary' nature of the communications seems to prevent the experimenter from accepting their full implication. This is noticeable when, for instance, he or she publishes the literal text of some of those transcendental messages followed by his/her own personal interpretation, which visibly aims to minimize the full impact of the 'revolutionary' piece of information. In such cases, it is the interpretation that is influenced by the experimenter's own mental modeling.

Chapter 7

Some Similar Concepts and Special Features that Occur in Rio do Tempo's and Other ITC Communications

Brief Remarks on the Concepts of Spirit and the Spiritual

Matter is equivalent to energy. Or we could go further and affirm without being proven wrong that what we perceive as matter is actually energy. And from a transcendental point of view, we can very rightly say that every living being is a spiritual being because it is animated by the life principle (vital energy or spirit), that some call 'Prana', 'Chi', 'élan vital', and so on. It cannot be seen, touched or accurately described but it indisputably exists. We, as a life form, are simultaneously its manifestations and its witnesses.

Sadly, the word 'spiritual' is often used to describe certain people, situations or anything at all without much thought or criteria. We will hear that somebody is 'spiritual', while another person is 'materialistic', and although in this particular case the use of the words might be justified because they basically refer to the interests of the people concerned, in my opinion it is still a deficient terminology. Conversely, a sacred mountain is 'spiritual', while a mound of land where one grows food is merely something 'material' and of no importance. The sacred tree of Japan, the gingko tree, in India the peepal tree, and particularly the Bo tree under which, as tradition has it, the Buddha attained enlightenment are all sacred, while the apple tree or the tomato plant or any other vegetable that sustains life will be something of no significance – a 'material' vegetable to eat or discard. For those who like to define things as 'spiritual' or as 'materialistic', as it has become fashionable in this so-called New

Age – a movement incidentally that has done much to degrade real spirituality – the horse, the lion, the deer, the bee, indeed all animals, all plants and most humans will not be considered 'spiritual' perhaps because, putting it in a simplistic way, they do not take meditation retreats, do not listen to Bach, do not know Buddhism exists, etc. Criteria such as these are used to define spirituality by New Age Western people who do not realize that animals and definitely plants are perfectly in tune with life itself. It is this being in tune with life that represents true spirituality if we wish to use a word that has become debased.

If and when the expression 'spiritual' is used with religious connotations it becomes even more dubious and incorrect because it is more restrictive. In whatever way it is used, it is always judgmental, therefore reduced and limited by human preconceptions. Consequently, in my view, to use the word 'spiritual' to describe the next world carries no real meaning because we are also spiritual here in this world, as is the tree, the lion, the fish, the insects, etc. It is life that is spiritual. Wherever there is life there is spirit. They are one and the same thing.

Masanobu Fukuoka, an illuminated sage with whom I had the privilege of sharing some time when I lived in Japan, says that 'he searches for God who does not know Him. Animals and children do not search for God.' (Fukuoka, 1987).

Rio do Tempo have told me in one of their communications that 'animals and plants are more aware of the existence of our [their] world than humans.'

At this point, I believe it is not necessary to say that practically none of the mental models we have fashioned for the next world fit into what the communicators describe as their domain of reality, which seems to be truly holistic. They describe their world as all encompassing: 'This is Rio de todo, this is Rio de todos, this is Rio do Tempo!' (This is the River of the whole. This is the River of all. This is Rio do Tempo!) And as a continuation of life, very simply a continuation of life without any of the 'intellectual' speculations humans are so keen about. Frederic Myers said practically the same about the falsity of the mental constructs that we, humans, create about the next world in the *The Road to Immortality*.

The Concept of a Station in the Next World

Human mental models appear to be the reason why the idea of a station in the next world is disturbing for many people. But don't we, in this less developed world, have many stations and all kinds of agencies, some of them highly sophisticated like NASA? It is only natural and befitting that there will also be stations in the next world, which is 'a world very similar to yours [ours]', as Rio do Tempo once described it to me, although much more developed since it is the next step in the ladder of existence. The communicators tell us that they send contacts to our and other physical worlds from these stations or agencies. They also say that this is an extremely difficult process. We could certainly speculate on the nature of these stations from which practically all the most developed contacts of different researchers throughout the world appear to originate. Maybe they use high technology (of a different kind from ours) combined perhaps with mental and psychic energy (maybe other kinds of energies also) with generous motivation, with love and a desire to help us. The communicators maintain that indeed they study, invent, develop and use special devices and technological equipment. We are also told that higher beings supervise their work in these transmitting centers (Locher and Harsch, 1995).

The communicators have also told us that with sufficient training almost everybody in their world can make EVP contacts (microphone recordings) with us while DRV, transimages, computer texts, etc. have to be channeled through a station. Even in the mediumistic communications quoted in Chapter 2, which announced the advent of Instrumental Transcommunication, such highly sophisticated devices are clearly referred to.

There will be those who will put forward the idea that such material concepts must rather apply to thought forms brought by the communicators from our world into the next world, and are to be considered 'contaminated' by earthly mental models. Others will say they are symbolic expressions, metaphors used to transmit to us something we can understand, etc. To accept such reasoning we would have to be able to prove that matter does not belong in the next level of life, and of course we cannot do this especially because we are told by Rio do Tempo and other communicators that their world is also a physical world. As such, it is legitimate to consider that such things as equipment and stations equally exist in the next physical world that some of us like to call the 'spirit world'.

Human Prejudices Are Responsible for the Rejection of Information Received From the Communicators

The 'spirit world' is an expression commonly used in opposition to the concept of a 'physical world' [our planet Earth] very much in the Cartesian, dualistic way which many years ago science showed us to be incorrect. Alas, for those who think in terms of the old, obsolete dichotomy body/spirit, how can there be 'stations' in the next world?

As a matter of fact, the main prejudice against the existence of stations and other things, such as proper devices in the next world, arises from our predominant conditioning. Even people who are disposed to accept the idea of life after death, whether in a religious context or not, seem reluctant to accept the idea of a station. We humans create mental models for almost everything, including the idea of a life after death (assuming we take the idea seriously). And that is how mental models work – they permeate and dominate our thinking, even though we may be unaware of them.

An important obstacle to the acceptance of the existence of stations and other material things our invisible friends frequently mention in their communications, from the early times of Friedrich Jürgenson, derives from the fact that some people seem to think of the next world as a world constructed by thought, a mental world, and if that is so, how could there be real stations in such a world? For people who say these things, everything in a world of thought is simply a mental creation, a thought form of what we have in this world, and therefore illusory. This perspective is even more anthropomorphic than the commonly held view that humans are the center of our world, and the rest of creation is inferior and subservient to us, because it also perceives the next world as a domain of reality dependent on the creative mental capacities of deceased humans, one into which we will transplant our preferences when we die. Such a view deprives the next level of life of its autonomy. At the request of a friend, I once asked Rio do Tempo if their world was a world of thought and to this they replied, 'Our world is closer to the truth than your world [i.e. Earth].'

I think one of the main reasons why some people have diffi-culty in accepting the 'material' (physical) conceptions put forward by the communicators has to do with the idea of the visible and undeniable destruction of the body. This apparently dreadful circumstance will impress into their minds the idea that if something survives it has to be thought. Certainly thought will survive as will almost everything else – the information field pertaining to each living being survives, as stated by the commu-nicators on many occasions to different experimenters. But we are also told by the communicators that they 'also have a body, a much more beautiful, much more flexible body made of a kind of electricity,' as Rio do Tempo once said to me. Interestingly, Emanuel Swedenborg, a remarkable scientist, the great Swedish mystic and visionary of the 17th century, in one of his many descriptions of the death process and of the feelings of people when they pass through it, already mentioned this body: '...and they get very surprised for finding themselves in a body and in all senses the one they had in the world…' (Swedenborg, 1853).

Sadly, the majority of people will also have great trouble in understanding how plants, for instance, can also survive, and naturally microbes, bacteria, viruses, etc. This predominantly anthropomorphic mental attitude is based upon two main beliefs – firstly, in considering that thought, the intellectual activity of the mind, is the property of the human species. Thus, some will speak of 'survival of the mind'. Secondly, in thinking of matter as we know and experience it. Both reflections are definitely narrow-minded and arrogant and can easily be dismissed by a zoologist, an enlightened botanist (Bose, 1902, 1913, 1926) and a quantum physicist. Naturally, every living being, from the humblest blade of grass to the most intelligent, developed human being, must possess an information field that allows it to live its own life and to survive, sometimes under the most appalling adverse conditions. Without a 'mind' or information field (congenital and acquired) nothing could live, since in order to be able to survive, every living being needs 'thought' or the capacity to decide how to act in the face of the circumstances (natural and otherwise).

Frederic Myers allegedly described some of the living conditions in the next levels of existence, as we discussed in previous chapters. In Luxembourg, the high entity whom the experimenters called the 'Technician' said that the depiction of the afterlife given by Myers, although not exact, was the most approximate to the reality of the worlds beyond. The latter affirms that almost all of the next worlds are 'worlds of form,' and consequently where there is form there has to be substance (matter). The nature of this matter, or more appropriately, of the 'matters' of the next worlds, will be different from ours but will nevertheless be matter. In addition, when Myers says 'shape or form,' he implicitly means that they are illusory. All matter – ours or the much finer matter of the next worlds – is impermanent and illusory, and it will all disappear by whatever means. Perhaps in the next levels of life – and it would mean the same if I said of consciousness – the dissolution of matter is not so disruptive and repulsive (particularly as in the case of the matter that constitutes our own and other animals' bodies) as in our own world but it will still mean the termination/transformation and disappearance of that matter. There will come a point in the ladder of existence when consciousness will 'have no need to express itself in a shape, however tenuous, however fine,' but it will take 'aeons of time within the mystery of timelessness,' as Myers puts it.

A Common Pattern for the Next World Emerges

The existence of stations in the next world, where the contacts apparently originate, is in fact one of Jürgenson's main conclusions based upon the communications he received, and he frequently refers to such 'stations' or 'agencies' in his books (Jürgenson, 1964, 1967, 1968). Says Jürgenson: 'All contacts that are started with our sphere are subject to the supervision of a so-called 'Central Research Station' and evidently cannot take place without the latter's mediation.' In his book, *Voices from the Space*, he also maintains that no radio recordings can be made without the cooperation of a mediator in the next world. In his case, the mediator was Lena, a deceased friend of his childhood.

In *Breakthrough*, Dr. Konstantin Raudive reports that when he started the radio recording method, the Latvian Group in the next world told him that they would help him with his work. And on page 174 he goes on to confirm that, 'The astonishing conception that 'other-worldly' transmitting stations exist emerges quite clearly from many of the voices' statements. Information received indicates that there are various groups of voice-entities who operate their own stations.' Among other references to the Portuguese Group in my own recordings, there is a voice that once remarked, 'Hoje não vêm os Portugueses à Estação Rio do Tempo.' (Today the Portuguese will not come to

Timestream Station.) The obvious parallel to Raudive's information needs no further explanation.

As I mentioned in Chapter 2, one of my main communicators, Carlos de Almeida, communicated initially with Maggy and Jules Harsch-Fischbach in Luxembourg and announced the existence of the Portuguese Group some years before I started my own experimentation. To the present day I have not had any personal contact with Maggy and Jules, except for the exchange of short pieces of correspondence at the beginning of my own research, and therefore it seems that this event significantly corroborates the information received since Jürgenson and Raudive about the existence of stations in the next world. Moreover, Dr. Luísa Alcântara, the fairly recent ITC experimenter who lives in Aveiro, Portugal, started to receive DRV contacts from a group that also identified themselves as Rio do Tempo and in many instances their voices sound very similar to the voices I receive in my own studio (Cardoso, 2007).

Besides Maggy and Jules, other experimenters have reported receiving communications from transmitting stations in the next world, as it was, for example, the case of the late Adolf Homes and Fritz Malkhoff, both of them from Germany.

Advanced contacts channeled through a station that allow for better, two-sided and more comprehensible communications seem to entail the supervision and concurrence of higher beings that decide when and who may talk. As I mentioned somewhere else in the book, I have several DRV recordings where a voice, different from the voice that was communicating with me, interrupts whoever is speaking from the other side to say, 'You may continue,' or 'It is over,' and other things to this effect. At other times an imposing voice will suddenly break into the communication to direct the trend of the conversation. The same situation is described in Théo Locher's and Maggy Harsch's book on the Luxembourg phenomena that reports on events which, in some instances, are strikingly similar to my own experiences. Luísa

Alcântara witnessed a similar occurrence during one of her DRV communications. Her sister-in-law, who was also present in her studio on this occasion, asked to speak with her mother and the anomalous voice replied to her with, 'She [the sister-in-law's mother] is listening to everything but she has no permission... [to speak]' (Alcântara, 2008). It is as if these contacts that allow for such an astounding exploration of the next level of life have to be carefully monitored and controlled, possibly in order not to allow them to be debased.

More Remarkable Similarities – the Radar, the Spaceship, Flying in Space

The description of all the similarities between the content of Rio do Tempo's communications and especially Friedrich Jürgenson's but also other experimenters' contacts could cover many pages, but I shall present only a few examples.

In his books, Jürgenson comments extensively on the puzzling 'Radar', seemingly an intriguing 'device' his own communicators frequently referred to. In one of those passages he says:

As soon as I was able to establish a radio contact with Lena's help, I could be sure that I was being observed by her via a kind of radar screen. Lena did not only see my body sitting in front of the radio receiver, but she was able to read my thoughts at the same time and even before I had thought them out completely.

I can fully corroborate the information conveyed by Jürgenson using the same precise words for both situations – seeing my body and room and reading my thoughts before I had completed them – which have happened frequently in my own experimentation.

Furthermore, during the first months of my ITC work the

word 'Radar' could be heard several times in the DRV contacts and it used to puzzle me and my friend Carlos Fernández who, at the time, was often present at my house during Rio do Tempo's transmissions. Neither of us knew then that Jürgenson had had similar experiences because it was only years later, when I lived in Lyon, that an anonymous friend of the ITC Journal kindly offered me the private translation into English of Jürgenson's *Sprechfunk mit Verstorbenen* (Voice Transmissions with the Deceased) from which I have extensively quoted in the last chapter. Among other statements about the radar, Friedrich Jürgenson goes on to say that

In such cases of these direct contacts I only had to pose my questions mentally after which I received an answer immediately via the radio directly to my tape. These direct recordings provided the best proof of how the radar method succeeded flawlessly in executing the connecting function.

One day in Lyon I had a very exciting experience of the same nature as the ones described by Friedrich Jürgenson. This was a period when Rio do Tempo would sometimes not want me to have my mobile phone connected while they worked with the radios, practicing with their voices in my studio; but on other times they said that it did not affect their work [to have my mobile on]. So, every time I needed to use my mobile phone when the radios were on, I used to go upstairs (my studio in Lyon was at the second floor of the house) and ask Rio do Tempo if I could connect it. On one of those evenings I started to perform the routine and went upstairs but the moment I opened the door of the room, before I could articulate any sound or even construct the sentence in my mind properly, a clear radio voice that I could understand directly without any doubt, said 'Hoje tu podes ligar o telemóvel.' (Today you can connect your mobile phone.) Professor David Fontana, who was in my house on that particular occasion, can corroborate what I affirm because I immediately went downstairs to the lounge and, quite shaken, told him what had just happened. Naturally, given the circumstances, I could not, unfortunately, record the communicator's remarks.

An extremely interesting occurrence happened eight days after Jürgenson's death. There is a published report of his post-mortem contact in Luxembourg with the Harsch-Fischbach couple and a German investigator, Dr. Ralph Determeyer, during which he apparently expressed his great joy at being able to speak with those present and comment on his new existence. The published record of what he said then states:

Good afternoon, my friends! Here it is Friedrich Jürgenson speaking! I thank you for coming. **Naturally it is another type of connection, a radar, that has now been constructed here by our friends in our side.** It is a great joy for me to be able to speak today. See, this is how it is: a small bird; its life; its perception (viewpoint)... the small man, who is a prisoner of his daily routine environment... man suffocates man.
(Schäfer, 1989, 1993)

References to the 'radar' are also to be found in Dr. Raudive's *Breakthrough*.

Friedrich Jürgenson mentions extensively what he calls the 'spirit ship' used by his communicators 'to fly through space and time'. He reports that words to this effect were heard and recorded by him often. In one of the transcriptions from his recordings appears, 'Hugo is examining moon satellites... Hugo is making space flights...' etc. Hugo was his dear deceased friend who also acted as his gardener.

Gabriella Alvisi, in her *Dimensione Radiosa* (1983), talks a lot about the 'nave' (ship) which her communicators told her they use in their 'flights'; they even mentioned it in one of the songs that they sometimes sang during her ITC experiments. 'Siamo dalla nave qua.' (We are here in the ship) sings the happy voice that I have listened to. These communications happened dozens of years before I started my own ITC work and received communications from the Group called Rio do Tempo. It is fascinating to note that the similarities still happen so many years later, for the word 'nave' (in Portuguese 'nave' is mostly used to designate a spaceship) was very frequent at the beginning of my own DRV contacts. When I once asked if they traveled in a 'nave', my 'transpartner' replied in the odd syntax construction frequently used by the communicators, 'Fez-se essa nave foi para aqui só!' (That spaceship was built for here only!) This voice is included in the CD.

At the beginning of my DRV work in 1998, the communicators used to make frequent references to 'being in space'; 'We entered space'; 'We are speaking from space', and say many other similar things. Once they said to me in a singing, joyful tone, 'Havemos de andar no espaço juntos!' (We will be in the space together...), and a voice that identified itself as my grandmother's replied to my question as to who was I speaking with, 'É a tua avó que fala do espaço.' (It is your grandmother speaking from space).

It is rather delicate to deal with concepts such as the 'radar' and the 'spaceship' for it can induce the readers to make a parallel with our own radar or spaceship technology and, therefore, it could be misleading. I am not implying that the communicators are not referring to instruments for they could very well be; I just wish to clarify that their 'radar' and their 'spaceship' are not our radar or our spaceship. If they really mean instruments they would necessarily be made of a finer, more vibrational matter than our own, as it is perhaps the case with their bodies, that we are unable to see.

I will quote Myers about the death process:

The secret of death is to be found in the rate of speed at which the outer shell vibrates. For instance, a human being is primarily aware of the visible world about him because his body is traveling at its particular rate of speed. Alter the timing of your physical form, and the earth, men, women and all material objects, will vanish for you as you vanish for them. Death therefore means merely a change of speed. For the purpose of this change a temporary dislocation is necessary, for the soul must pass from one body traveling at a certain vibration to another traveling at a different rate or time.

And he says in another passage,

He is a kingdom (the discarnate being) bounded by what would seem to have the appearance of a veil. It has a curious elasticity. I mean we differ from the kingdom to which I have alluded [the human body] in that we can alter at will the shape of this very subtle material or fluid. We differ in many other aspects. Our surroundings are of a metetheric character. You may ask me to define this. It is exceedingly difficult. But I think I may say that it contains atoms of the very finest kind. They pass through your coarser matter. They belong to another state altogether.

Thus, it could be that the invisible communicators really mean devices when they speak of their 'radar' or 'spaceship' but it could also be that by using such terms they try to convey to us concepts that we can understand. Or it can be both – perhaps their devices are of such a different nature from ours that they use words we can recognize to call them and give us a hint at their functioning. I suppose this question – if they mean devices or procedures of whatever nature – should remain open until the communicators are able (or allowed) to convey to us a more helpful explanation. I firmly believe that mind-openness is an important attitude when we deal with such complex areas of research. It would be a symptom of arrogance to definitely pass judgment on these concepts, for we have no way of knowing for sure what they mean. It is certainly legitimate to question these types of statements but perhaps not legitimate to come to conclusions about them.

Another of these very striking, closely connected similarities concerns one of the most extraordinary voices received by Maggy and Jules Harsch-Fischbach, later identified as the voice of the high entity that they called the 'Technician'. I quote again from the book on the Luxembourg phenomena:

The signal indicative of the contacts was made by a strange, 'hammered' voice that sounded as if produced by a computer and which was reminiscent of the clear voice of a child. This 'computer voice' pronounced numbers as if trying through this to establish the contact with us and to stabilize it.

The experimenters attributed this computer-like voice to the Technician.

At the beginning of my own experimentation, during the first weeks of the DRV, a strange, masculine, mechanical voice could be heard frequently in my house at different hours of the day, coming directly from the loudspeaker of one of the radios, very loud and clear, pronouncing interminable strings of numbers, sometimes in English, other times in Spanish, for as long as over 30 minutes, always with the same monotonous cadence of a computer, without interruption or failure. Whether or not this voice was related to the so-called 'Number Stations' of Akin Fernandez and 'The Conet Project' will, I suppose, remain a mystery. The truth is that, unlike what happened with the communicators proper, I never managed to get a reply from the computer-like voice that repeated the strings of numbers. But it also must be said that when the DRV communications got established and consolidated, that voice was never again heard in my house.

The communicator, identified as Carlos de Almeida, had said that the 'Robot would speak' and from the beginning of April until the beginning of June 1998 this strange voice could be heard several times, although another masculine voice, less machine-like, could also be heard counting during these first months of the DRV.

Nevertheless, I must say that to me the robotic voice trans-mitted by one of my radios (at the time an old valve radio) does not sound like the Technician's voice which I have listened to in some of the Harsch-Fischbachs' recordings; however, a very similar voice to the Technician's voice appeared recorded on one of my tapes as a short EVP while I was experimenting. But I suppose the high entity known as the Technician can produce many different voices. This would justify what Rio do Tempo once told me about communications with the high entity whom I longed to speak with – 'But you have spoken with him many times!' Thus, this remark hypothetically means that the Technician used completely different voices from the one that investigators well-acquainted with the Luxembourg work recognize as his peculiar voice. It makes a lot of sense when we consider that the Technician is supposed to be a very high entity and consequently capable of what, for us, are feats of an unimag-inable nature.

Chapter 8

The 'Bridge', the Tower, the Group-Soul and the Extraordinary Capacities of the Next World

The Construction of the 'Bridge' Between This World and the Next World

Leaving aside the ancient metaphor of the connecting 'bridge' between the worlds, that is part of any occult tradition or religion anywhere in the world, we shall deal with the 'bridge' in terms of ITC contacts. There are abundant references in the already extensive literature of this discipline to the so-called 'bridge' between this and the next world as discussed in previous chapters.

Friedrich Jürgenson refers repeatedly to the 'bridge', as does Konstantin Raudive. Adolf Homes and the Harsch-Fischbachs extensively report about the 'bridge' in their own contacts and it seems that this bridge is a requisite for the most sophisticated forms of communication. In Luxembourg, for instance, there were several complex technological systems of contact which the communicators called 'bridges' – the Burton Bridge, the GA 1, the Eurosignal Bridge. But it is Gabriella Alvisi, the late Italian ITC researcher, who in my opinion gives one of the best definitions of the 'bridge' – seemingly so important in ITC contacts – that I have seen published. Writes Alvisi:

From the moment when the 'bridge' (this is a definition inserted by the communicators in the magnetic tapes of all experimenters) is established, the understanding capacity of the earthly creature supersedes 'the very near veil' that has always been represented by mystery, going from an initial feeling of uncertainty to a supreme conviction which was ultimately attained by those who possess authentic faculties considered paranormal but which in reality are a part of the laws that govern human nature. (Alvisi, 1983)

What does the 'bridge' consist of? Since we have no precise, detailed information from the communicators on the nature of the 'ITC Bridge', we can only speculate about it. Besides the evident allegory used by humans throughout their history to describe the possibility of establishing contacts with another level of existence, it is legitimate to think of it as perhaps a complex system of resonance or affinity between the communicators, the experimenters and the environment. A system that would also include the electronic devices used for the contacts, all linked in a very special (to us mysterious) way, through subtle physical-mental-psychical-spiritual interconnections and interaction.

The Tower

In October 1998, strange information was yielded by my communicators that proved years later to be highly meaningful. A powerful masculine voice started a communication with 'Torre, Torre, é o Rio do Tempo!' (Tower, Tower, it is Rio do Tempo!) (See CD). I have to confess that the word 'Torre' really puzzled me at that time for I could attribute no proper meaning to it (in the context of the next world) and it seemed bizarre, to say the least, that they would speak to towers. It was only years later speaking with Professor Senkowski, that I found out that Maggy and Jules Harsch-Fischbach of Luxembourg had also received communications related to a tower in the context of *Zeitstrom* (the contacts were in German) i.e., Timestream or Rio do Tempo.

There are a number of instances of corresponding information conveyed at different times or simultaneously to different ITC researchers who in some cases not only did not know each other but did not know about each other, also, as was my own case. I find that this situation is of utmost importance because, apparently, it implies that in the next dimension of life there is a common pattern, something that clearly identifies itself with distinctive, often physical features, as happened with the 'Tower'. One of the anomalous images received by the Luxembourg group on April 21, 1987, displayed a kind of construction that resembled a tower where work related to the communications with our world allegedly took place (Locher and Harsch ibid, 1989). The image was described as follows by the high entity they had called the Technician:

> In the construction shown works P. K., a well known communicator. Here it is also located the transmission station from where transcommunication with the Earth is realized.

Interestingly, Professor Ernst Senkowski, in the first edition of his work *Instrumentelle Trasnkommunikation* (1989), refers to a text that Count Mancini-Spinucci of Fermo showed him – this was the original of Count Mancini's mother's handwritten report of a mediumistic session in Milan on May 22, 1934 and it said:

> The promise can be kept when/if exists the possibility to keep it, and this evening I have for you only this: the loving greeting of the SCIENTIST of the TOWER, who comes to you and supports you and through my mediation says: Brother in work, work is long and arduous, because the calculation does not always work out and is erased; but if the belief is strong, then science is sure/positive. Listen: In the tower there is a mysterious and overwhelming collection of discoveries which the men on earth one day will be able to recognize, and within short, i.e., when the point of time will have come and will have come easily, the prize will be the new theory of the

discovery in the field of electromagnetism. I will bring you the exact description of a new apparatus which you easily will be able to realize with perfect earthly calculations.

It concerns a work of which my friends have spoken to you already: the easy receiving of the thoughts of the deceased, our deceased in another life, who are always alive around you. They do not always have the possibility to speak like during their lifetime, but they always have the possibility to think. Their speech consists of thoughts. If thoughts consist of vibrations and the vibrations move the molecules of the cosmos: why then should it not be possible to gather these vibrations and bring them onto a disc. Imprinted in this disc, could man then not perfectly recognize the thoughts of the one that had left the earth?

With this force, with this invention, the great doubt, the great fear of the end, of the real end of man will be erased from the plan, and there will be a major re-orientation in the field of religion, since religion consists of doubts and of fear. This new belief, that addresses man's conscience, will not see the monk's garb and not the priest's stole, but only the word of the one who has relation to the 'returned' deity. This will be when the activity of the brothers, who shape the brains of men themselves like potter's earth, will be able/allowed to easily explain and convey to you these scientific conceptions, and you will be able to pass them on – slowly modified – by yourselves. However, as on our side, cautious reticence is required, so silence is the secret of mystery, but it is the door and the key that inaugurates the rays.

And so be always over you the blessing of the unknown forces/powers, which/who at all times watch around everybody who believes and hopes it be so. The times will not pass by; the suns will not pass by before this will come back and slowly begin. Because the work must progress slowly, the work of penetrating must be cautious. Though it is not necessary for you who believe and whose belief is firm, the work must nevertheless be slow and cautious for the others who shall believe, and there must be no fear of lack of determination. But I will come and meet you again, prior to what has to be the termination; thereafter I will initiate you in the study and describing of details.

(Remark: it was suggested that the Scientist of the Tower could be Rudolf Steiner). (Translation from the full text published in German)

What could be more indicative of the forthcoming ITC way of contacting the next world than '…the prize will be the new theory of the discovery in the field of electro magnetism,' a discovery within the 'mysterious and overwhelming collection of discoveries' contained in the Tower?

The Group-Soul

In brief, the occult tradition has it that the Group-Soul is a matrix that aggregates all members of the same species, and that there is a different group-soul for each species (Gettings, 1986).

In *The Road to Immortality*, Frederic Myers described the group-soul as the fundamental basis of life in the next worlds but his explanation is much more comprehensive than the one put across by the occult tradition. Says Myers:

The actual construction of the group-soul must be clearly visualized. Its spirit feeds, with life and mental light, certain plants, trees, flowers, birds, insects, fish, beasts, men and women; representatives of living creatures in varying states of evolution. It inspires souls who are on various planes, various levels of consciousness in the After-Death. It feeds, also, creatures on other planets. For the spirit must gather a harvest of experience in every form. Gradually these intelligences evolve and merge… There maybe contained within that spirit twenty souls, a hundred souls, a thousand souls. The number varies. It is different for each man...

The readers will be able to listen on the CD to a segment where Carlos de Almeida says loudly and clearly, at the end of a long communication in which he also speaks to somebody called Pierre, 'Vai ser uma verdade a alcançar p'ra haver para aqui luz, oh Pierre liga o circuito posto aí, é um sonho meu!... Vocês vejam lá o circuito e as instalações de luz ... [undecipherable]...' (It will be a truth to reach to have light here. Oh Pierre, connect the circuit placed there, it is a dream of mine! You check the circuit and the light installations... [Undecipherable]...') And he continues: '...Ele não vem e ao meu grupo desço, vou à alma! É o edifício do Tempo, é o hemiciclo do Tempo...' (...He does not come and I go down to my group. I go to the soul! It is the edifice of Time [Timestream]. It is the hemicycle of Time...)

The content of this communication is remarkable from all points of view as we will see next. To begin with, there is a reference to the 'connection of circuits' and to 'the light installations', meaning very possibly electricity circuits. He could very well be speaking of my own house where I had a lot of electrical anomalies and malfunctioning of electrical equipment when the DRV contacts started. In my opinion, the main question is – which circuits was Carlos de Almeida referring to? Was it our circuits or perhaps the communicators' circuits installed in my house, of whose existence we cannot be aware? He probably meant the latter. But there is still a possibility that he may be speaking of circuits in their own world. And here we have one more issue that must remain open because we have no way of finding a reasonable explanation for these questions. Then, there is the remarkable, clear reference to the Group-Soul, as we have seen in Chapter 6. The explicit mention of his 'group' in direct connection to his 'soul' makes of it a landmark among ITC communications because it seems to be the manifest confirmation of the reality of this important 'social' pillar in the next world, the Group-Soul. And lastly, because of the exotic syntax of the sentence, 'It will be a truth to reach to have light here...', a common feature of many ITC communications that we will examine in the next chapters, as well as what seems to be the symbolic use of the word 'light'. Furthermore, the seat of Timestream Station was described in communications received by other researchers, namely the Harsch-Fischbachs, as a hemicycle. There is not much more we could aim for as matching information!

It all prompted me to ponder on Myers' words again, this time in regard to the Group-Soul.

...he [any human being], however, may not leave it [the Fifth plane] for the Sixth plane until the Group-Soul is complete, until those other souls, necessary to this design woven in the tapestry of eternity, have also attained to this level of consciousness. Some may still be far behind. But while in this state of being, he becomes aware of the emotional life of all the more primitive souls who inhabit denser and denser matter and, yet, belong to his group. He becomes aware, in short, of all the parts of the great body which his spirit, or the Unifying Principle, feeds with its Light. He realizes the subconscious life of the flower, the insect, the bird, the beast, all those forms which are connected with the governor of his being, that Light from Above.

The notion of the Group-Soul is also implied in several of Rio do Tempo's statements, as for instance in the case of the voice that reprehended my father when he identified himself with his full name. As readers will recall from Chapter 4, that authoritative voice demanded that my father identified himself with 'Rio do Tempo' only. Or when, at the end of a particularly long and successful transmission, I thanked 'those who helped and made this contact possible,' and an anomalous voice immediately replied 'Everybody helped!' On another occasion a voice, different from the voices that normally claim to be João Cardoso, which I described more extensively in another chapter, said, 'Está a falar o teu Pai em conjunto!' (It is your father speaking all together!) I found the most striking and unexpected similarity to my DRV in a clear, intelligible DRV that my good friend Dr. Carlo Trajna, one of the most knowledgeable international researchers in this field, sent me a few months ago together with a set of samples of his own recordings. The voice, which I carefully listened to and keep in my computer files, says: 'Insieme tua voce sarai di qua.' (Literal translation: **together** your voice will be here.) I avail myself of this opportunity to thank Carlo Trajna for his friendship and encouragement throughout the years and for having shared with me many examples of his own excellent results.

Rio do Tempo's communicators also say that animals and plants collaborate in their projects and in their endeavors to make ITC contacts possible. Consequently, this is still another circumstance that falls within the scope of the Group-Soul as described by Myers and confirmed by my communicators.

To the best of my knowledge, there are no explicit references to the Group-Soul in the literature concerning the messages of other ITC experimenters, although many refer extensively to their group in the world beyond as is the case of Gabriella Alvisi amongst others. One of Hildegard Schäfer's communicators used a very beautiful expression that I particularly like. In the course of a contact, Schäfer said that she hoped the invisible partners could hear her, and the voice replied, 'Of course, you are in my soul!' (Schäfer ibid, 1993, p. 266). Professor Ernst Senkowski, who was himself a successful ITC experimenter, received years ago a very interesting EVP voice that stated: 'Deine Geistfamilie vermittelt ihre Kunde.' (Your spirit-family transmits their information.) And I shall again cite Myers speaking about the Group-

Soul, '…So, when I talk of my spiritual forbears I do not speak of my physical ancestors, I speak of those soul-ancestors who are bound to me by one spirit…'

Extraordinary Capacities Seem to Pertain to the Next Level of Existence

The amazingly transforming power of death, as Friedrich Jürgenson called it, and the extraordinary capacities that belong to the next world and become available to all beings that live in it, are manifest in most of the communications we receive. Humans who speak from the next world seem to be profoundly transformed, although not in the sense that the concept of 'beautiful angels floating on clouds' would imply. They are transformed in a thorough, deeply understanding and truly developed way.

Through death, an important expansion of consciousness seems to be attained, and this expansion is just one of the many similarities that exist between reports of NDEs (Near Death Experiences) and ITC communications. Says Jürgenson:

> This is not to say that all dead persons are suddenly transformed into pure angels. The decisive transformation that took place in the psyche of the deceased only depends to a certain extent on the deliverance from their frail human bodies. The most significant role is played by the influence of their dimension outside time and space, a synchronicity that affords the dead the great advantage of direct perception. The practical results of this timeless perception can only be perceived with difficulty from our perspective, or not at all for most of us. (Jürgenson ibid, 1967)

Some other extraordinary capacities available to all who cross the threshold of death are, according to my own communicators, 'to be able to be in two places at the same time,' or 'to travel with thought,' 'to communicate by telepathy with each other, with people on Earth, and with animals and plants,' and certainly many others which they cannot describe to us for we would not understand them.

When I once asked Rio do Tempo if these extraordinary capacities were acquired through the death process, they replied that they pertain to their world and are available to all who live in it. The parallel to Jürgenson's statement is clear but it is also important to emphasize that I received the information from Rio do Tempo long before I read Jürgenson's statement; something I only did a couple of years ago.

Chapter 9

The Founding of the ITC Journal

The Founding of the ITC Journal

In July 1999 my term of office in Galicia finished and I was transferred to Lyon in France. Rio do Tempo's communications by DRV had gained an impressive rhythm and I could listen to my dear friends almost every evening. By this time, my father, who died in 1993, and my brother Luis had already communicated several times together with my grandmother, as it happened, who had died twenty years before this date and also Nisha, my beloved Doberman dog, deceased in 1995. Other people, that I cannot recall knowing, had spoken and given their names, most of them in Portuguese. The communicators gave the impression of a tremendous amount of development work at the Station in order to enable the communications.

The idea that, for my part, I should also contribute to this effort in a more effective way had been in my mind for some time but I really did not know what I could do for this purpose. With the help of Carlos Fernández, Rio do Tempo's website was already on line, but I thought that was not enough and felt the compelling need to help more with their terrific effort. It seemed to me that their extraordinary feat – sometimes the contact could be maintained for over two hours – could not be destined for me only; it had to have a much wider and more general reach.

One day the idea of starting a publication came into my head. It would be another completely new adventure for me for I knew absolutely nothing about the editing and publishing business. Nevertheless, I knew that I would like this publication to bring ITC phenomena to international attention in a serious way. There was nothing in the world specific about ITC at that time and I wanted to start a magazine that would assemble the most knowledgeable international experts in the field and that would also be a forum for the exchange of experiences of experimenters from all over the world. The main features of the ITC Journal appeared clearly in my head – it should be a serious magazine and should be international. The spirit of the communications was certainly international and in their content there was no place for selfish pettiness or obsolete nationalism. I thought it should be in three languages – in Portuguese, in homage to the earthly origin of the majority of the communicators; in Spanish because it was in Galicia, Spain that they had communicated and in English because of the international reach of the language nowadays.

The idea was in my mind and in my heart but it had come at a very complicated time – I was going to France in a very short time and how could I edit a publication in a country that I only knew from having visited it a few times in the past? The whole project seemed unfeasible, at least at that time, but stubbornly I did not give up and continued thinking that it needed to be done urgently. I started contacting people and asking for their support – Professor Ernst Senkowski, one of the world's most knowledgeable experts in the field of ITC; Dr. Adrian Klein who was then the coordinator of the now unfortunately dissolved International Network for Instrumental Transcommunication (INIT), a man with many connections in this area while I was a total newcomer; Professor David Fontana, whom I had not yet met but to whom I would write regularly giving him news of my contacts with Rio do Tempo; Dr. Hernani Guimarães Andrade, the great Brazilian expert on all kinds of psychical phenomena, who never failed me with the appropriate word at the right time and did a lot to support my enthusiasm; Dr. Carlo Trajna, about whom we spoke in the previous chapter, although we never met personally, accompanied me since the very first days of my experimentation showing great interest and always providing excellent advice with great generosity and wisdom; Paolo Presi, an extremely well-informed researcher, always supportive and helpful; and a very dear friend in France, whom I never met but was unlimitedly kind and helpful – Pierre Théry, who died after the publication of the very first issues of the Journal, but with whom I still had a couple of wonderful telephone conversations when I arrived in Lyon. There were others; Carlos Luz and Cristina Rocha from Brazil were always there for me with their encouraging words; Father François Brune, Jacques Blanc-Garin and his wife Monique with whom I had many contacts especially while I lived in France; Maggy and Jules Harsch-Fischbach were welcoming and friendly in the long writings that constituted our exchange of correspondence at that time. They were particularly important to me because the account of their experiences was, in some way, the key that opened this fascinating field of research for me. Later their support was expressed through a series of articles published in the first issues of the Journal.

Nevertheless, the main question remained open – how to carry on with the project in practical terms? Once again, Carlos Fernández was instrumental because, on my proposal, he agreed to taking care of in Spain all the issues related to the publishing of the journal and such pertinent details as finding a convenient publishing house, posting the publication to the subscribers (at that time, non-existent), writing the envelopes and taking everything to the post office, etc. From my side I would write papers on my experiments and their results, request other researchers and experts to do the same, putting forward their opinions and experiences with ITC phenomena, collect and arrange all the texts, translate most of them, and send them to him in Spain where they would be printed for reasons of costs and practical convenience. Carlos, although a little perplexed, finally agreed and together we started the exciting new venture, notwithstanding the fact that we did not know very well how to proceed I must confess. Carlos is a technically-minded person and so he learned how to lay out the journal – work that he did from the very beginning until a couple of years ago when his professional duties as a journalist and the resultant time constraints prevented him from continuing to do it.

There were other friends, some of whom I never met, that kindly supported the new project and I apologize for not mentioning them all but I hereby express my sincere recognition to everybody for the general enthusiastic support we received when I launched the adventurous new proposal.

And so in the year 2000, issue number one of the ITC Journal saw the light of the day. I was already in France but often used to come back to my house in beautiful Galicia that I so missed. Carlos had kept the Journal for me there, and I have to admit that it was a real thrill to see that very first issue in print with a beautiful cover designed by a good friend, the Portuguese painter and poet António Afonso, who generously got involved with the making of the covers. The first three issues were designed by António.

This had been another concern – who would do the covers? Neither Carlos nor I knew how to set up a proper cover for a publication and I refused to have one of those monotonous covers that you see on all the so-called 'serious' journals. They are always pale blue, pale cream or brick color with black letters, and so on – very boring I have to admit, and most of the times dull and inelegantly plain, too. No, I certainly did not like that and besides I also wanted to convey a little message through the cover of the Journal. The first message was that serious subjects do not have to be monotonous and to consider that something is frivolous because it depicts beautiful flowers, for instance, is in my opinion a silly prejudice. Thus, as I enjoy going against the flow especially when I feel the current 'flow' is stagnant, I decided the covers of the Journal should be lively and colorful, calling people's attention, whenever possible, to little things that otherwise would go unnoticed.

I like photography although, unfortunately, I do not have

enough time to practice it – a necessity if you wish to achieve good quality work – so I decided to use some of my own photographs in the Journal. Since then I have used those for most of the covers of the Journal and I hope to have passed on the message that things do not have to be plain and boring in order to be serious and deep.

Little by little, with some sacrifice because the translations are a difficult, time consuming job, the ITC Journal became well established and gained a good reputation. It has subscribers from all corners of the world and words of praise and support are generously conveyed to me by the many people interested in ITC research and results.

To edit the ITC Journal has been a most gratifying experience. It has been a difficult even a heavy task sometimes, because I have had to do almost everything for the Journal, from translating and editing texts written in several different languages into English and Spanish, to carrying heavy packages containing the envelopes for the subscribers on my shoulders to take them to the post office, sometimes over a lengthy walking distance, and many other things. For a few years I had to pay for them too because the money of the subscriptions was not enough to pay for the printing and mailing costs.

But I have been fortunate as well to have had the help and support of a number of admirable people. As I said, my friend Carlos Fernández helped me ever since we started the journal and throughout the years that I lived in France. Professor David Fontana helped me with the editing of many papers in English, normally written by non-English speaking authors, and with a lot of other precious advice about the best way to edit a journal, something at which he is proficient. Professor Ernst Senkowski is always there to help me in the most generous manner, promptly and efficiently, whenever I call on him because of some difficulties with ITC references, or I need to know details of the 'classical' experimenters' experiences, or physics issues, etc. My

Italian friends – Enrico Marabini, Paolo Presi, Michele Dinicastro and Daniele Gullà – have never failed me whenever I have some doubts about the cases reported in the specialized literature or when sophisticated analyses are needed of the interesting material sent to the Journal by unknown people who apparently experienced ITC events, and many other things. For the last three years, Ann Harrison has replaced Carlos Fernández (now too busy with his professional work) in the laborious job of doing the layout of the journal. She does wonderful work of a professional quality and she also has helped me with the revision of English texts, a most necessary work because very few of the people who contribute to the Journal are proficient in English, yet their work has been impeccably presented to the readers mostly on account of the excellent editing done by Professor Fontana, and lately also through the always available, good-willing contribution of Ann Harrison.

The ITC Journal Research Center

Late in the year 2004, David Fontana and Carlos Fernández enthusiastically gave their generous support and co-operation to another project dear to my heart – the ITC Journal Research Center. There was a particularly strong reason behind my enthusiasm for the Center. When I lived in the United States I was fortunate to meet, in the course of my professional capacity, a wonderful lady, a collaborator who became a very good friend. She is a kind, sensitive, intelligent and committed lady; she is also brave and generous and has had plenty of opportunity to prove it. The last 30 years of her life have been what we call in our world a 'rosary of calamities'. The last and greatest of them all was the death of her only two children and her unborn grandson. These sad losses happened one after the other as a result of car accidents. Even before these major misfortunes, she and her family had lost all that they had built up with great work and effort in one of the former Portuguese colonies. From a sound social and financial situation, they were suddenly left in very strained circumstances.

My friend's soul was broken after the death of her children, but she continued to undertake everything with great courage and dignity, keeping the serenity and profound generosity that made her worry more about others in need than about herself. When her second child and her unborn grandson died I feared for her emotional and psychological balance and for the repercussions that such dramatic events would have in her already so devastated life. However, she continued to follow her path, with a bereaved heart but a smiling face, always attending to others.

Around this period I had started my ITC experimentation and had obtained my first results. The continuation and strengthening of the contacts prompted me to suggest and recommend to her that she too start her own experiments to try and possibly establish contact with her deceased children. The idea filled her with emotion and expectation, but to the present time she has not yet started this work. Although separated by the Atlantic Ocean we exchange frequent correspondence. She used to tell me, 'I will visit you one day in your house and then I will ask you to teach me the techniques so that I can start experimenting myself, for I need to feel that I know what I am doing.' In vain, I assured her that there is no secret to the procedures and that they are all easy to learn and execute. I sent her personalized information on ITC techniques, detailed descriptions, and photocopies of research papers. I have recommended books, but I have not been able to change her attitude. It is this wonderful friend, this brave woman, as discreet in her sorrow as in everything else in her life, who was in reality the inspiration for the Seminars. As a result of our correspondence, I realized that there must be many other people like her who do not dare to take the first step in ITC experimentation on their own, and I thought I could perhaps help them. This is how the idea of the ITC Seminars was born in my mind and in my heart.

With the idea of the seminars came the idea of the Center, of an institution to sponsor these and other initiatives that I thought would also be important for everybody involved in the experimental work with ITC and to the people at large, because I firmly believe that the door, potentially open to everybody through the transcendental electronic contacts, is of utmost importance to humans and can change the world if correctly and fully understood.

One of the requisites to accomplish this goal, in the times in which we live, is of course the recognition by science of their veracity. Therefore, scientific examination and confirmation of the evidence yielded by ITC is primary and urgently needed. One of the newly established ITC Journal Research Center objectives would be the scientific study of the objective materials provided by ITC experimentation.

I had started receiving numerous invitations to give presentations on Rio do Tempo's contacts. One of these was in London, the Gwen Tate Memorial Lecture to the SPR, and at this conference a new era started.

Among the fairly numerous public present at the lecture was a nice, discreet, strong-minded looking gentleman, who came to meet and congratulate me at the end. Mr. Knowles expressed his interest in my work and said that he could be of the disposition to finance research into ITC. Greatly encouraged by this interest, I then compiled a research proposal together with Professor David Fontana, who chaired my lecture at the SPR, outlining how the grant would help us to take this work forward. After vetting by the appropriate SPR committee, the proposal was then submitted to Mr. Knowles, in competition with one other shortlisted proposal, and he duly selected it for his approval.

The seminars started in 2006. The first one was very well attended and we had to refuse a couple of applications because I thought that more than 15 students would not be advisable as those attending would not fully benefit from it. Luisa Alcântara greatly helped me in this new task. She came from Aveiro in Portugal, where she lives, 250 km away from Vigo, generously giving me her help and support with the preparation of the courses.

The first Seminar was particularly difficult because, during the month of August, when it took place, we in Galicia experienced one of the most devastating periods of her modern history – the great forest fires that burned to the bone over ten percent of the land. Those fires, huge and uncontrollable, were everywhere and also all around my house forcing us to be vigilant and scared 24 hours a day, without any kind of rest for eleven days. One night the fire came into my own garden and it was a terrible feeling seeing the garden engulfed by the flames, being forced by the police to evacuate the house with the maid and the dogs and not knowing when everything would be finished, what I would find, including the condition of Rio do Tempo's recorded tapes and materials. This was certainly one of the most frightening times of my life together with the terrible experience I lived through in New Delhi, India, in the aftermath of Indira Gandhi's assassination by her Sikh body guards.

Therefore, a bare ten days after the nightmare of the fires finished, the first Seminar on ITC techniques took place at an office rented purposely for them at the beginning of the year. My state of fatigue was extreme and I am sure I could only find the strength to carry on with the scheduled event, and not cancel it out as my body and mind urgently demanded, in the love I feel for my communicators. I knew and felt this was a project dear to their hearts, too. As I mentioned before, a communicator who identified himself as Carlos de Almeida had once told me, 'It is for humble people. It is to call upon love, [the] panacea of the world. It would be beautiful, would it not?' Nothing can better express the spirit of the seminars than this utterance.

Amazingly and totally unexpectedly, we had results right at the first seminar, which was held in Portuguese. These were in the shape of faint, short but audible EVP replies to the questions put by the participants to the invisible communicators. They were always pertinent to the question asked and a couple of the whispered voices were even articulated in Esperanto, the language that the couple of participants, both experts in Esperanto, had used to address them. One of these replies though, was not weak and it was not short considering that it was an EVP utterance like all the other ones. I shall briefly describe what happened because I believe it will be interesting for the reader.

One of the ladies present, Maria dos Anjos Gomes Antunes, accompanied by her husband and young daughter, asked the following question: 'Is anyone from Rio do Tempo Station listening to me?' When we rewound the tape and listened to the group's recordings (the students were assembled in groups of four or five people) there it was – a fairly loud and clear masculine voice that could be heard in-between the commercial tape music integrating dolphins and whales shrieking sounds of joy, used as the background noise, and said in three segments interspersed with slight pauses 'I am listening ... very low ... with great effort' (translation from the Portuguese). This was captured by another lady's tape recorder since Maria dos Anjos' recorder had not functioned when she spoke.

Many lessons could be learned from this occurrence, the most important of which is perhaps the fact that this lovely woman, who was deeply grieving for the death of her only son killed in a car crash, did not ask to speak with her son, something that perhaps reflects, on the one hand, her unselfishness, and on the other her concentration on the work, rather than a preoccupation with her own problems. The second lesson is that the work done at the Seminar was definitely harmonious group work, something that seems to be very agreeable to the communicators and beneficial for the contacts. The Group-Soul seems to be a concept of great strength in the next world as I had the opportunity of pointing out in the previous chapter.

The conclusions I have just drawn reflect my personal views and understanding of the communication process but, as I stressed before, they are by no means supposed to be the teachings of the communicators. The phrases between apostrophes that I have transcribed and quoted are solely those directly and audibly pronounced by the communicators. I am extremely keen on this because I do not wish to be taken as their ethical herald; I am simply a scribe of their communications to all of us.

There were other seminars and we had results in all of them. Little voices of low amplitude but, nevertheless, real whispered voices that conveyed meaningful replies appeared, registered on the digital recorders and computer hard discs of the participants, all pertinent to the questions asked or to the situation at the seminar. I deliberately did not do any particular personal recording during the courses neither did I put any questions to the invisible communicators.

The work continues and I sincerely hope that all those genuinely interested in the next dimension of life may benefit from these seminars and achieve their own direct contacts for, in my opinion, they are one of the most sublime experiences anybody can have in this world.

Chapter 10

The Role of the Experimenter

The Human Partner

At this point in my story I believe that readers who are not familiar with the subject will be curious and interested to receive information about the methods they can use to start their own experimentation. I will deal with these in the next chapter. I would also like to assure them that although the idea of experimenting with ITC may appear complex and rather intimidating, there is really nothing to fear. The simplest form of ITC experimentation, namely EVP (Electronic Voice Phenomenon) is accessible and appropriate for everyone, both in terms of technical expertise and financial outlay. One initial recommendation I consider to be of great importance is to strongly advise readers and potential ITC experimenters to try and read at least a few of the most representative works about ITC history, methods and research (enumerated in the bibliography), starting naturally with the works of the great pioneers Friedrich Jürgenson and Konstantin Raudive that I consider indispensable.

Naturally, investigators with advanced knowledge of electronics and acoustics may wish to try and develop devices and techniques of their own, as did the Austrian engineer Franz Seidl who invented what is known as the 'psychophone', an electronic device that he hoped would improve the quality of the voices received, which many experimenters have used since then, apparently with good results. The Swiss physicist Professor Alex Schneider, who worked in close cooperation with Konstantin Raudive, also invented the so-called diode[5] method (Schneider, 1970, in Appendices to *Breakthrough*), and more recent researchers, such as Hans Otto König, have also developed their own devices, often under the guidance of their communicators. The various devices concerned all appear to have produced good results, but I must reiterate that in my own experience, and that of the many people with whom I have worked, ITC contacts do not depend upon the precise technical conditions available or upon the sophistication of the equipment used. Very basic equipment appears as effective in producing results as much more elaborate pieces of hardware.

I will not go into details here of all the sophisticated devices referred to above, but the bibliography at the end of the book provides suitable references for the technically minded who may wish to go more deeply into the subject. I must confess that I have no theory as to how these devices could enhance the reception of communications – if indeed they do – but for those who may wish to puzzle over this I strongly recommend Hildegard Schäfer's book, *Brücke Zwischen Diesseits und Jenseits*, which provides detailed descriptions of some of the best known of them, together with diagrams that will enable any technically conversant reader who wishes to try and duplicate some of them, to do so. Sadly, the book has not yet been translated into English, although I think that there are some private translations posted on the Internet.

It will perhaps already be clear to readers that my personal conviction is that it is not possible from our side to create a highly sophisticated technical system that will decisively improve the quality of contacts, unless such a system is adequate for the communicators' own needs, and fits the progress of their own work. Therefore, I do remain open to the idea that certain electronic systems may be more conducive to the needs of certain communicators.

Whenever I discuss ITC methodology at seminars and lectures, I always emphasize that it is the invisible communicators, and not the researchers, who do the most difficult part of the work. It is the communicators who have to produce apparently human voices that can interact with us, which we can understand most of the time, and that can convey meaningful information often unknown to the experimenter. We, on Earth, only create the conditions for these voices to be heard and recorded. Hans Otto König puts it very well when he says '...if we believe that we can direct [control] these contacts with the Beyond we are making a big mistake because the communicators say *'We create the contact''* (König, 2007). There must be endless unknown factors that play a role in the fascinating and myste- rious process that allows the communications to become audible, but we are far from discovering what they are. To speak of *synergy* between the communicators, the investigators and the equipment might seem relevant here, and I believe that it possibly plays a significant role in the process. However, we cannot explore this proposition for lack of knowledge and infor- mation about the ways that it involves. Consequently, we would have to enter too far into speculation, and I think it is better to leave the matter open, at least for now.

I suppose we should ask here whether or not there must be some form of initial interaction between the mind of the commu- nicator(s) and the mind of the experimenter if the phenomena are to develop, and whether or not some form of compatibility must exist between the two for this interaction to take place (reference is, in fact, often made by communicators to a 'Bridge' as we discussed in more detail in Chapter 8). In trying to answer this, I have to say that to the best of my knowledge there are no examples of real ITC communications (i.e. communications containing a meaningful interchange of ideas) arising solely from a request by the experimenter and without any previous relationship between him or her and the communicators, although such connection does not have to necessarily go back to Earth times together. A previous interaction of some kind between communicators and experimenters seems to be essential, even though this interaction may be a difficult and time-consuming process, producing only poor results over a number of years before there is any discernible improvement in voice reception (Cardoso 2006). In my opinion, affinity between the two sides is an indispensable condition for the contacts to happen. It is difficult to define with precision which expression such relationship may assume but we have already spoken about the Group-Soul and that is the best way to look at it. The will and the desire to effect communications and a deep longing for the contact from both sides are other conditions that offer a good basis to think about this important issue.

We have to accept that the communicator takes the active role and the experimenter the passive role in producing communications, and this holds true even if we take the view that the experimenter in some way makes an active contribution through the action of his/her mind on the radio or the recorder through the operation of some form of unconscious psychokinesis. Even if psychokinesis allows the mind of the experimenter to be a co-creator of the anomalous voices, and of images and computer texts in this way, the ability to use the human mind's resources (and perhaps other environmental factors) in what must be an extremely complex and synergetic way comes from the communicators themselves.

It is well known anecdotally that under some circumstances highly sensitive electronic equipment, such as computers, can be influenced by the mind of the user through some form of unconscious anomalous action (Radin, 2006), and it is true that although some people have a permanently smooth relationship with their equipment others have what seems to be a permanently disturbed one, in which everything electrical that they touch seems to malfunction, break, go berserk, etc. Given this situation, it is perhaps reasonable to suppose that the mind as well as the mood of the experimenter can influence the process of communication under the intelligent influence and the 'direction', if we may call it that, of the communicators. At this point it seems pertinent to recall what I said in previous chapters about the state of tranquility that Rio do Tempo communicators have frequently told me I should ideally experience if I am to help in their ITC work.

When I mentioned earlier the possibility that the mind of the experimenter may play some part in the successful receipt of ITC communications through a form of psychokinesis, I must make it clear that this should not be taken to mean that I support the premise advanced by some parapsychologists that the communications are 'created' solely through the psychokinetic action of the mind of the experimenter on the electronic equipment. I would like to quote here a knowledgeable researcher of the voice phenomenon, indeed one of the pioneers of this research, Peter Bander, who was present at Dr. Raudive's tests in Great Britain, and who was also a successful EVP experimenter. Commenting on the theory that the voices are due to the subconscious mind of the experimenter, Dr. Bander insists that, although it is possible that the subconscious may send out mental impulses, 'they would be unlikely to register as something so artificial as human speech. There is a substantial difference between a thought-form and its conversion into the spoken word. The latter is a conscious action which is often none too easy and can require a conscious effort.' (*Voices from the Tapes*, 1973, p. 20). Dr. Bander also takes the view that even the proverbial chimpanzee playing randomly at the piano would have 'a far better mathematical chance of playing all of Beethoven's sonatas than a single thought form has of manifesting itself through electronic impulses and recording itself as human speech' (ibid page 21).

Besides Peter Bander's pertinent observations, I will add that it is very unlikely that some of the odd grammar constructions often used by the communicators exist in the linguistic mental structure of the experimenter which corroborates fully what Peter Bander says. I will give an example of one of my own DRV contacts. Lady was one of my beloved Doberman dogs, one of

Surya's and Nisha's puppies, as I mentioned before. She had a chronic, difficult heart condition and because of it I sometimes had to withdraw from my recording studio, even when a contact with the communicators had been established, in order to attend to her. On one of those occasions I apologized to my invisible interlocutors saying that I regretted having had to leave the studio but Lady was not well. Their immediate reply through DRV was, 'Every time she dies from our part you do not have the right to be sad!' To who would such a grammar construction – 'Every time she dies...' – occur? For we undoubtedly think and speak about death as an event that happens only once in a lifetime. Lady died four days later.

When I once questioned Rio do Tempo as to why their voices were sometimes very clear, other times distorted, and on yet other occasions inaudible, their interesting reply was, 'We don't know.' In my view, the fluctuations in the quality and reception of ITC voices are due not to any possible psychokinetic action of the experimenter but in some degree to the 'uncertainty' that we are told by physicists operates at the quantum (the sub-atomic) level that underlies all the physical matter that makes up our world. It seems pertinent to report here that at the beginning of my experimentation with the DRV, sometimes the communicators replied to my questions, asking if it was Rio do Tempo speaking, with the words, 'Yes, it is. The voice just drifted there [i.e. here],' and 'It is Rio do Tempo speaking to Europe.' Since 'just drifted there' or 'speaking to Europe' seem to refer to the general quality of the information contained in the communications, we could perhaps speculate on the possibility that the experimenter produces what in quantum mechanics is called the 'Observer Effect' – i.e. the very fact of his or her keen interest in listening to the voices somehow 'transforms' the 'wave' so that the signal (information) it carries becomes available and audible to us.

'Wave' is perhaps an inappropriate term with which to

describe the carrier used by the communicators to transmit their thoughts to us, but at present we have no information that would allow us to describe it in a more appropriate way.

Another highly significant example of the 'uncertainty' of the conditions that I believe belong to the communication process is the communicators' reply, at the end of 2007, to my enquiry as to who was actually speaking. Their reply was: 'Falamos de Rio do Tempo e tu serás Vigo!' (We are speaking from Rio do Tempo and you will be [must be] Vigo!) See CD. Note the lack of certainty about my identity. Similar incidents to this have happened in other circumstances. For example, the communicators have occasionally asked at the beginning of a DRV contact: 'Who are you?', when Carlos Fernández and I were speaking with them, as described in Chapter 4. However, on yet other occasions they have seemed clear as to my identity, announcing through DRV at the end of a communication, 'Rio do Tempo transmitiu p'ra Anabela Cardoso, Anabela Cardoso de Portugal.' (Rio do Tempo transmitted for Anabela Cardoso, Anabela Cardoso of Portugal.)

I believe that instead of regarding these two communications as contradictory, we should view them as complementary in the light of my above speculations on the operation of 'uncertainty'. We simply do not know how ITC communications reach us, and these speculations are no more than speculations, since the subject of 'uncertainty' has never featured in any of the replies I have received from the communicators to any of my questions on the nature of the media used by them to effect their communications. Nevertheless, the communicating entities do seem to recognize the important part played by the interactions respectively between the electronic equipment used, the human experimenter, and the communicators themselves. The researchers in Luxembourg reported being informed that (literal translation), 'The psychic domain [of the experimenter] represents up to 1/5 of the technically supported contacts while 4/5 come from us. When we do experiences with a medium, the psychic domain [of the medium] extends to 4/5,' (Locher and Harsch, 1995). The communicators then went on to insist that their aim is to free their communications completely from human influence, and in 1988 they declared, again in Luxembourg, that 'the use of human psychic faculties is no longer necessary for the new experiences,' (Locher and Harsch ibid).

Much has been said, and a lot more has been guessed, about the possible role of 'mediumship' in ITC communications. I will not get into that discussion which I find stale, because if I did I would be doing exactly the same thing that I reproach others for doing, i.e., I would be guessing.

To say proper things about this subject we would have to define first what mediumship is, and this would be a very difficult task to start with. Personally, I prefer the use of the words 'telepathic contact', although they probably mean the same thing. The potential of telepathic contact, or mediumship, or psychic information, or whatever other name we wish to give that very little known feature, is something that must be present in all life forms. Speaking from my own experience, based upon the many conversations I have had on the subject with large numbers of different people, as well as from my observation of people's, as well as of animals' reactions, it is a quality common to everybody. Psychic awareness, as I prefer to call it, seems to be a condition to life that may manifest itself in many different ways. In animals it appears as something more natural and taken for granted by humans, an attitude that has always puzzled me.

Acute psychic awareness is mostly used by non-human animals to provide for their living and/or emotional needs. We just have to recall the recent case of the 2006 tsunami in Asia, when not one single elephant perished from it; or the countless cases of dogs and other pets that find their way back home, or to their human friends, through indescribable dangers and extremely long and complicated distances. Rupert Sheldrake wrote a book about it (Sheldrake, 1999), but such stories are of popular knowledge and confirmation everywhere in the world. Human psychic faculties are perhaps less obvious than animal ones, and I suppose that the reason why our species lost close contact with such an important life attribute (indeed indispensable, for instance, for hunters as well as the hunted in the animal kingdom) is related to the development of the intellect, and other tools that apparently compensate for it. There are many published works about indigenous peoples' and animals' psychic feats that give striking examples of what I am trying to say, but I will not go over them here since they are not in the scope of this book (e. g. Bozzano, 1941; Schmidt, 1970). I believe that these attributes, the so-called psychic faculties, even if not in as sharp a condition as they must once have been, can be directed into any direction one is interested in.

I am not implying that individual cases of extraordinary psychic capacities do not exist. There are rare cases of individuals who have given proof, since early childhood, of possessing a natural link to the Invisible; a deep psychic awareness that must have belonged also to humankind. They are classified as 'human phenomena', and the esoteric literature is full of accounts of their feats, admittedly not all of them proven beyond any reasonable doubt. Nevertheless, to my knowledge, none of those highly psychically developed individuals became ITC experimenters with outstanding results. There are not even known cases of classical mediums experimenting in ITC, and certainly none who have attained notable results. Furthermore, not one of the most successful ITC experimenters falls within the category of exceptional psychics. On the other hand, many of them (e.g. the Harsch-Fischbachs, Adolf Homes, Bacci among others,) are defined as possessing strong mediumistic capacities. But there is no striking proof of these capacities prior to their experimentation. Parapsychologists try to justify their results by calling them people with strong psychic capacities, which for me sounds like an obscurum per obscurius statement. Such an affirmation cannot be proven and, therefore, it does not carry much weight. It is possible that close contact with another dimension, a realm more of the psyche than the one we live in, has somehow transformed or enriched those experimenters through the resonance process. This is, in my view, a much stronger possibility.

Readers will find that I occasionally mention, throughout the book, that I perceived subjectively pieces of information from Rio do Tempo, and I wish to clarify what I mean when I make such affirmations. As a matter of fact this is correct but it does not imply that I am a psychic human phenomenon. When, puzzled by the impressive amount of contacts with Rio do Tempo, I once asked Carlos de Almeida what was the psychic process that allowed for those contacts, he replied, 'Não há processo.' (There is no process.) On another occasion he said that I was normal. Nevertheless, I really have a strong telepathic connection to my communicators that permits me to subjectively perceive their information whenever necessary. I wish to emphasize that readers who do not consider themselves capable of this type of connection need not be discouraged from attempting the contact with another dimension of life. It may happen naturally through love and the strengthening of the relationship with your own communicators.

To me, this telepathic perception of Rio do Tempo's information happened for the first time in the year 2000, when I was already in Lyon, and it was a wonderful surprise that filled me with excitement and joy! This is a psychic bond possibly of the same type of the one that unites a mother to her baby, or two inseparable friends, two very attached lovers, a dedicated and loving dog to his human companion or vice versa, and so on. We should remember, after all, that people such as William O'Neil, who had such a decisive role in the development of the Spiricom, was just a normally successful healer when he started working with George Meek. Through the Spiricom process he naturally developed what are considered by many researchers his 'strong psychic and mediumistic capabilities' to the point that, as reported, he would frequently see Dr. Mueller's materialization and would speak with him as if he were present. However, if we read Fuller's book conscientiously, we verify that all this happened <u>after</u> he got involved in the Spiricom project (Fuller, 1985). Let us look at it this way – O'Neil's psychic capacities were necessary to accomplish the breakthrough achieved with the Spiricom, therefore they developed! Once again the communicators surely play a determinant role in these processes.

Psychological Factors in the Experimenter

Naturally, as in any other activity, and very especially in an activity of such a subtle and delicate nature as ITC that involves contacts with an invisible dimension unknown to the majority of humankind, the individuals interested in 'The opening of the road beyond time' (as my own communicators once called the process of communication) should preferably possess some specific psychological characteristics, the most important of which is that they are stable people with their feet firmly on the ground.

It is also necessary that they have no fear, because fear can jeopardize the whole process, not so much because it inhibits the communicators but because it inhibits the human experimenter and can prevent him or her from being focused and interested in the communication. As a consequence, the fluid interaction between communicator and experimenter (at both the conscious and unconscious levels) that we spoke about earlier will not easily take place. Fear can also produce in the experimenter irrational feelings and inappropriate perceptions. In truth, there is nothing to fear from our deceased loved ones, who we dearly loved when they were alive, or from other unknown people or entities that address us amicably and insist that they are speaking from another level of existence – an inspiring, beautiful dimension of life far more advanced than our own.

I will give an example that illustrates what I wish to convey about the dangers fuelled by fear. A few years ago I received frequent emails from a woman in the USA who I did not know, requesting my help in getting rid of, as she described it, 'abusive, threatening and extremely rude communicators that are transforming my [her] life into a real misery.' I agreed to her request that I listen to a few of the recordings she copied for me that contained, according to her, 'the most injurious words of abuse with sexual connotations'. I listened very carefully to the samples she sent me but could not find a single word or even whisper in them. It was all random noise; they contained no speech of any kind! Apparently she had been 'hearing' in the noise things that were clearly not there.

The above example relates to a phenomenon that we will discuss in more detail when we come to the section on listening to the recordings. Known as 'pareidolia', the phenomenon refers to the tendency of some people not only to claim they hear voices in indistinct sounds but actually to claim that they can distinguish the 'words' involved. Their unconscious minds are, therefore, projecting meaning into sounds that have no meaning, something that can happen particularly in circumstances such as fear, and that may reflect a psychologically rather unstable state of mind. We also know from psychological experiments that when told there are voices contained in 'white noise', many individuals will claim that they 'hear' them. Such is the power of suggestion and expectation.

Stories about undesirable communicators abound, but fortunately, as I said earlier, I have never encountered any hostile or threatening voices in my years of research. However, I am not entirely ruling out the possibility of hostile communicators. It may be that in ITC, as in many areas of life, the rule that 'like attracts like' prevails. In that case, provided our intentions towards the contacts are good and pure, we have nothing to fear.

We should keep in mind that the next dimension is a world more advanced than ours – a characteristic of anything that is superior in an evolutionary sequence – and that in that subtle, ethereal, psychic world our thoughts, motivation and the real goals of our actions are transparent to the communicators. From the time of Friedrich Jürgenson, there have been frequent, common testimonies from ITC experimenters that emphasize the fact that the communicators seem 'to know all their thoughts' (a likelihood that also seems to be born out by the content of some communicators' remarks). This certainly appears to be true, as we do not appear able to deceive them.

Carlos de Almeida once gave me an extremely interesting explanation about the 'mysterious' way through which our dear friends, the communicators, are able to know our thoughts. I had asked him how they could hear my voice because I naturally assumed that, being in another dimension, they could not physically hear me when I spoke inside my studio. His reply, which readers can hear in the CD, clearly said, 'É ritmo. Nós sabemos quando o seguimos.' (It is rhythm. We know when we follow it.) But my question continues to puzzle me. What rhythm was Carlos de Almeida speaking about? Was it the brain rhythm? It most likely was because the brain rhythm is constituted by electrical impulses that the communicators from another dimension may well be able to read easily. Nevertheless, we cannot be sure. Was he perhaps speaking about some other rhythm not yet discovered by science? Interestingly, when a few days later I asked him if by "rhythm" he meant the rhythm of thought, his reply, unfortunately not clear beyond doubt, seemed to confirm this proposition. This is another fascinating issue that must remain open until we have the knowledge and the conditions to deal with it.

Deep interest in the contacts – in this case in ITC contacts, but it could be in classical mediumship (telepathic contact) or in any form of art, for example, or in inventions or new discoveries, sport feats etc. – is, in my view, a condition of utmost signifi-cance. Profound, relentless interest is an essential condition for making what one longs for to come true. From it inspiration arises, if we speak of artistic expression; ITC contacts if we speak of contacts with another dimension through electronic means; mediumship if we speak of telepathic contacts with the Unseen; finding their way home through several hundreds of kilometers if we speak of dogs in search of their beloved friends or territory etc. These accomplishments are all of the same nature; they belong to the realm of the psyche.

There is a transcendental communication, which I cannot immediately recall the reference to, which says about classical mediumship being something to the effect of: 'it is the interest of the medium that makes the contacts happen.' I think this is basically true, and therefore I classify real interest as the main desirable requisite for an experimenter. It should naturally be assumed that when I say interest, I mean an intense desire that comes from the heart and from the soul, not ambition or frivolous curiosity, speculation, pride in the contacts, or so forth. It is also possible that this interest, which admittedly may involve a strong component of love, needs to be shared by the communicating entities if the contacts are to prove successful. But in this case we are already speaking of the extremely important role played by the so-called 'resonance' (empathy) between the communicating entities and the receiving human experimenter, as we have seen before.

It is also very important that experimenters are not people of an obsessive nature or of obsessive tendencies. One of the real dangers of ITC experimentation, especially for deeply bereaved people, is that it can create in them an obsession with ITC work that may lead them to devote all their full and exclusive attention to this work at the expense of the mundane earthly tasks, which, after all, are the main purpose of our lives on Earth.

Another type of obsession has to do with the results produced by ITC experiments. It is fairly common for experimenters to become worried about the quality of their results. This can lead either to an obsessive focus upon these results and an extreme preoccupation with attempts to improve them at any cost (something that apparently is not easily within our reach), with the consequent disruption of daily life, or to the experimenter's increasing disappointment and consequent abandonment of the research. Both situations are obviously undesirable.

As previously made clear, a state of tranquility seems to be of the utmost importance in ITC work. My invisible partners have told me innumerable times, 'We need you to be always very tranquil.' In Grosseto, at the studio of Marcello Bacci, the communicators declared (literal translation), 'It is necessary to be in the disposition to discover serious things with the greatest serenity.' But it is difficult to keep inner tranquility in extraordinary situations such as those we experience in ITC exploration. It is natural for the human mind to feel overwhelmed by emotion and awe when the individual discovers the possibility of speaking directly with deceased people and other entities from another level of existence. This is certainly a life-changing experience, but it is important to keep one's balance and a certain sense of detachment. An attitude of serene expectation is perhaps the most suitable in order to help the communicators in their work, and therefore the most suitable in attaining the desired results. Such an attitude will also help us to retain our capacity for critical judgment, and for rigor in scrutinizing all essential factors in a field where one can easily slip into a state of obsessive fanaticism.

The unbiased investigation of the contacts should represent our main goal. Our emotional stability is naturally important for us, and for our invisible friends, since an obsessive, disturbed person will not be of great help to the communicators. ITC work demands a joint effort between communicator and investigator, and neither has an easy role, as made clear by one of my main communicators, Carlos de Almeida, who some years ago warned me '…This is difficult for both!' This statement again brings to my mind the importance of synergy between all the known and unknown pieces involved in the ITC process.

The nature of the information (the 'serious things' as the communicators called them at Grosseto) that is conveyed to us as the contacts develop and a dialogue begins to take place demand from the human experimenter great open-mindedness. When the information from the communicators starts pouring in, it normally shatters the traditional mental patterns we grew up with. The late Professor Hans Bender is purported to have communicated through DRV with Adolf Homes saying, among many other interesting things, that we should: 'Free yourselves [ourselves] from the rigid attitude of tradition and open yourselves to the new forms of probability of a genuine system that I am now learning to know.'

It takes a strong mind, a free spirit and a lot of understanding to accept, for instance, that a plant or an animal can be more developed spiritually than a human, as Hans Otto König's communicators have said (see chapter 6). To give you an example of the real shattering of mental patterns or prejudices that ITC communications provoke in many of us, a Canadian subscriber to the ITC Journal cancelled his subscription because for him, 'There is no way humans and plants can be basically equal,' even if in a cosmic sense. 'Does the carrot I had for lunch today survive my eating it and does it transit into another world? Pure rubbish!' And this kind of attitude will probably be shared by the majority of people. Nevertheless, Rio do Tempo communicators confirm: 'Aqui no Rio do Tempo todos os seres são iguais.' (Here in Rio do Tempo all beings are equal.)

I sincerely believe that among other factors, many of them undefined so far, success in ITC experimentation is intimately related to the open-mindedness and creative thinking of the human partner. Interestingly, Adolf Homes and Friedrich

Malkhoff, after trying several recording methods, also came to the conclusion that, 'It is our experience that success does not depend so much on the equipment but on the willingness of the experimenter to open himself to the Unknown,' (Locher and Harsch, French edition, p. 102). These qualities allow him or her to accept things considered impossible from the point of view of our present day science or of the known principles of what is thought of as Natural Law. This genuine acceptance at a deep level of the mind will naturally contribute to the fluidity of the interaction between communicators, experimenter, and equipment. I normally like to emphasize the fact that our knowledge of Nature is necessarily conditioned by the epoch we live in. Our past is full of the dramatic stories of discoveries that resulted in their authors going to jail or being burnt at the stake because these discoveries contradicted the known natural laws of their time. Today these discoveries are considered self-evident and an integral part of the set of natural laws that we now know. We smile with a mixture of contempt and compassion when we recall those past times, forgetting that they repeat themselves over and over again today. In reality everything is part of the Natural Law, but regrettably our knowledge of this law is limited and incomplete to an extent at which we can only guess.

Returning to our discussion of the factors that, in my opinion, favor successful contacts, I consider that even the fact of accepting that the voices of intelligent communicators, who identify themselves as the deceased, may appear mysteriously recorded on magnetic tapes, or may speak with us through the radio, is indicative that the concerned person possesses a natural open-mindedness that will enable him or her to participate in successful experiments. I am very familiar with educated people in liberal, successful professions who cannot face such a suggestion, while others of humbler educational background can accept it without great difficulty. On the other hand, it is not the fact of 'believing' in these contacts that will guarantee results.

There are skeptics who became highly successful experimenters, e.g. Hans Otto König among others; skeptics who tell us that they started their own experiments with ITC voices exactly on account of their disbelief in the whole phenomenon, and of their determination to prove it fallacious. This is a very important point because it demonstrates that the phenomenon can happen independently from the beliefs of the experimenter, and I reckon that this is quite an uncommon situation in the world of the so-called paranormal. However, not all the skeptics who started experimenting to verify the phenomenon for themselves produce results. One of the well known characteristics of anomalous phenomena is their elusiveness and their random repeatability. I wonder once again if these characteristics will be related to the quantum probabilities of the sub-atomic world. Indeed, I think this is the field of knowledge where we should search for explanations for ITC, and I hope that quantum physicists will one day take up the challenge.

The experimenter should also give priority to the indispensable requisites of persistence and patience. Serious ITC work demands a great deal of time and all the patience one can find within oneself. In 1975, George Meek went to Sweden to meet Jürgenson who commented on his research:

> You have to have great dedication for this work... and there are four basic requirements. First, you must have time – plenty of it. Second, you must have patience – an incredible amount of it. Third, you must have money, money to assemble equipment, discard what doesn't work, and buy more to replace it. But the most important thing of all is the willingness to take ridicule and slander (Fuller, 1985).

It is now over 30 years later, and unfortunately this wise opinion still holds well, especially in the context of the willingness to take ridicule and slander. Later on, in 1980, one of Bacci's communicators replied to a question about how to obtain better voices by saying (literal translation): 'We try the most possible to insert ourselves, it is necessary patience.' Bacci comments on this advice as follows:

> This statement given to our Roman friend and collaborator will certainly be useful also for all who despair or endeavor enormously in establishing a bridge with the voices; indeed psychophony is chiefly constancy and patience. (Bacci, 1991).

In my personal case, patience has also been an indispensable requirement. For the last four or five years, at the request of the communicators, all my set of equipment has remained turned on night and day for lengthy periods, sometimes for more than 15 days in a row. During this time, I cannot work with my computer because the communicators inform me that the functioning of computers in the building greatly disturbs their work. Sometimes I cannot even use my mobile phone at home or in the garden (although there were periods in previous years when the communicators specifically requested two mobile phones to be permanently connected in the studio where they 'work' with the radios, a request they have now discontinued). In addition, they now request my physical presence in the studio for some time almost every day, although they are not communicating with me but are simply 'working'. To our senses – i.e. to all that is audible to us – this *working* consists of the repetition of strings of words often preceded and terminated by the same recurrent acoustic signal. The communicators have repeatedly said that they are researching ways to improve the communications, and on other occasions, in reply to my mental complaints, they have said, 'We are building an instrument to enable us to speak directly'; 'We are working to be able to speak directly without any hindrances'; 'We are working to be able to speak to anybody who is interested in the contact with our world', etc. (This information was also perceived by me mentally; it was not uttered.) Whenever I describe what my communicators call their 'work' which normally consists of what sound like long sequences of words, the concept of the so-called 'Conet Project' normally comes to my mind. However, and although I have only listened to a few examples posted on the Internet, to my knowledge the voices of the 'Conet Project' do not repeat 'somos mortos' (we are dead), 'todos mortos aqui' (all dead here), 'fala-te o Rio do Tempo' (it is Rio do Tempo speaking to you), 'somos todos Tempo' (we are all Time [Timestream]), 'Bela' [Anabela], 'todos Cardoso' (all Cardoso) 'tia' (auntie), 'tio' (uncle) 'thank you', commonly among a string of other often incomprehensible words. These words are spoken by voices that sound as if produced by a machine and their cadence is odd. But it is also true that they can suddenly interrupt their monotonous repetitions and unexpectedly reply to one of my insistent questions. This is what happened when I once begged the communicators to reply to me and confirm their identity. They said twice, as I mentioned above, 'Falamos de Rio do Tempo e tu serás Vigo!' (We are speaking from Rio do Tempo and you will be [must be] Vigo.) And on another occasion, in a similar situation, a slightly different voice from the one that was repeating the words, replied to me 'É teu pai!' (It is your father!). To me all this seems exactly what the communicators claim it to be, namely work – hard, intensive linguistic work. Otherwise, how could we make sense of a voice, albeit a voice of the same acoustic type as the one speaking, that intrudes into the string of repetitions the words 'usar a pontuação' (use punctuation)?

Other ITC researchers have received information from their communicators pointing out that the motivation of the experimenter is an important factor when it comes to the quality of results (Locher and Harsch, 1995). Apparently, one of the features of positive motivation is humility. In this, as in other aspects of ITC research, it is important to keep in mind that nothing should be singled out for individual appraisal because the holistic quality of life seems to operate very distinctly in this area. I mean that, although the motivation and humility of the human experimenter, for instance, might play an important role in the process, no individual qualities should be isolated from the general context and presented as a panacea or justification for the contacts. Everything is complementary and inter-connected to an extent that we are not able to grasp, but that I suspect goes beyond our most ambitious suppositions.

Chapter 11

Summary of the Techniques Used in ITC

The Beginning

ITC results normally start by brief and faint voices, often monosyllabic, commonly called EVP, VOT (voices on tape) or psychophonic voices. At the very beginning, when we started getting positive results, my main preoccupation was to find ways to improve the communication. Consequently, one of the recurrent questions I used to put to the communicators was, 'What can I do to improve the contacts, is there anything I can do?' and one of their interesting replies said, 'You can make contact this way.' This was a pertinent answer because, in my opinion, it implied that the EVP method is the best technique to start experimenting for any type of ITC contacts. Indeed the 'Technician' had said virtually the same in Luxembourg (Locher and Harsch, 1995), and to my knowledge all successful ITC experimenters started with the EVP method, a technique that in some cases they used for years (see Cardoso on Bacci, 2006).

Therefore, my main recommendation to all those interested in attempting ITC contacts is for them to start with the EVP method and stick to it, avoiding the temptation to jump from one thing to another without allowing sufficient time for proper exploration and consolidation of the EVP method and the results. Patience and persistence are two fundamental requisites for this work, which is exceedingly fascinating but also very demanding if you wish to carry it out to its utmost possibilities. One of the conclusions we can draw by now is that without the full involvement and commitment of the experimenter nothing of real value can be achieved in ITC work.

It seems that the EVP method is also very helpful for the

communicators themselves, for it allows them 'to get used to working with that particular experimenter on Earth,' (Locher and Harsch ibid).

I also inquired and received replies of a technical nature and, as I said, I always followed the communicators' advice to the utmost of my possibilities. Perhaps, to some extent, my ignorance on technical matters was even beneficial, for I never took anything for granted. I mean, a question that might have seemed absurd to technically knowledgeable people was not at all so for me and I would carry on with it. I have a background in humanities and no experience of, or even an inclination towards, technical matters. Besides, since I really do not care about appearances, I do not mind giving the impression of being silly, and so I would ask what were naïve questions, at least from a technical point of view. But I preferred to put forward naïve questions to acting with the slightest doubt. I suppose I always thought, from the very beginning, that their processes, including the technical ones, had nothing in common with our ways in whatever area. And indeed everything points to this.

If we analyze the famous bridges of contact, set up under the full guidance of the communicators in Luxembourg, for example, we realize that these complex systems assembled a number of our technical devices in very specific ways that do not make any sense from the point of view of our technical knowledge. It is, therefore, obvious that, although the technical equipment is indispensable for ITC communications, apparently the processes involved bear no relationship to our technological procedures. They are of a different order. They could also be adapted to the experimenter's physical, psychical, and mental world.

When I once asked Rio do Tempo why they would speak more frequently through one of the two identical Sony radios, their answer was 'Because that radio is the one you like best.' Amazingly this is indeed true. However, it must also be said that some time later they started to use the other Sony radio to produce their voices. This is a good example of what I like to emphasize during the seminars on ITC techniques – there is no definitive or established set of rules for Instrumental Transcommunication work.

Moreover, I believe the communicators use the technical devices differently with each experimenter and this is perhaps the reason why a 'technical bridge of contact', i.e. a certain set of equipment, will work for a group of experimenters and not for another experimenter or group of experimenters. The exceptions to this rule exist but are very rare (Locher and Harsch ibid).

My questions were about the radios, the tape recorder, the position of the devices in the room, the frequencies – they said that the frequencies are not important, although some are more suitable for their work, apparently as a consequence of the type of noise they produce – about the most appropriate hours for the experimental sessions, the phases of the moon, weather conditions, etc. During that period there was a fall of meteorites and I asked about its possible effects on the contacts. They replied with great difficulty, through a faint EVP, that it prevented their communications from taking place.

How to Start Experimenting

I believe it might be useful for those readers, who wish to try for themselves the wonderful adventure of communication with the next world, to be given some details of my personal experience in the field. Readers might also ask and be very interested in knowing what the basic conditions for the establishment of the contacts are. When we started to get positive results and I could speak with the communicators, although in an incipient way, I once asked Rio do Tempo: 'What conditions do we need to contact your world?' To this they replied: 'There are no conditions.' On another occasion, when I asked how I could best contribute to the improvement of the contacts, they replied, 'Contact us!' (I have already mentioned similar replies to similar questions in previous chapters, and this was due to the fact that I used to ask this question quite frequently in an attempt to find out what else I could do to help the communicators' enormous endeavors). These two replies from Rio do Tempo communicators could perhaps serve as guidelines for those who wish to start ITC experiments.

In addition, let me say that I don't believe ITC can be directed by manuals, as a friend of mine, who himself experiments with ITC, remarked to me the other day. Indeed, everything seems to indicate that the laws and rules of our world do not apply to this field of research. Thus, to attempt to systematize things would certainly be misleading and perhaps even dangerous because it might impair the contacts. For that reason, everything that I write here should be interpreted in the light of what is said above – the details I give are only the result of my personal experience.

Where and How to Record

The experimenter should choose a quiet corner of his or her house and set up the devices there. If there is a small group of friends willing to try the contact together I recommend that it should be done at the home of whoever has the best conditions. Ideal conditions are, in my opinion, the following: absence of disturbing noises, tranquility, environmental peace and a certain intimacy of the room itself. I mean that whenever possible the room should be distant from the main center of the house where there is agitation and people all the time and even guests. A small room will suffice.

You will then need a source of noise. In my case I used the 'white noise' of radios almost all the time; generally the 'white noise' of short wave radios, but I also used radios tuned in to AM 'white noise' and the so-called 'broadband' (see the description of a 'broadband' radio modification at the end of this chapter). I had and I still have old valve radios and powerful, sophisticated, modern short wave radios. It is frequently said that old valve radios are important in ITC work. However, Rio do Tempo answered my question about the type of radios best suited for ITC by saying that the very powerful, modern ones are best for DRV (Direct Radio Voices), but for EVP it seems that the 'white noise' of any radio is suitable.

The radios (one or several according to one's own possibilities) should be tuned into a 'white noise' of medium intensity – not too loud or harsh and not too low. The experimentation in EVP can be tried either with one radio only or with several, three or four let's say. If the reader wishes to use more than one radio producing 'white noise' simultaneously, each radio should be tuned to a different frequency in order to make the 'carrier wave' available to the communicators as rich as possible. According to the information received from Rio do Tempo, the exact frequencies are not important, though the short wave band is strongly recommended, especially for the DRV. I have tried recording with other sources of noise, and I have received EVP answers through them – radio emissions in foreign languages for example, running water from the tap, the sound of soft wind in the foliage, chants, the traffic noise, music and birds singing in the open air. But in my experience, it is the 'white noise' originating directly from radios (which I prefer to the 'white noise' previously recorded on audiotapes or CDs, the so-called 'canned noise') that provides the best conditions for our communicators' contacts. At least, and I like to emphasize this, it is the one that seemed to work best for me. We should keep in mind that this is the acoustic carrier which can potentially be used for the DRVs, and such condition plays an important role in my preference. I once tried the communication by EVP in a hotel room having as background noise only a trickle of water running from a tap, and asked my communicators if they could also communicate through this acoustic background. A clear but faint masculine voice replied to my question with, 'There is not enough noise.' But I have also recorded EVP voices that answered my questions without any background noise, although they were much fainter than the ones that appeared recorded on the tape when I used the 'white noise'. Clearly, noise plays a role in the process, although we cannot yet define its exact functions besides what seems to be its role as a carrier (Hartmann, 2008).

Recapping on what has just been said; the experimenter or experimenters should install the devices in a small, quiet room. I try to have my recording studios (and I have had several, since I used to move from country to country) facing north. This is perhaps not important but I mention it as my first results were obtained in my house in Spain, which is still my recording studio today, in a room oriented toward the North. He or she should then supply the source of background noise, sit down quietly, and ask questions into a tape or digital recorder left running from the beginning to the end of the recording session. The brand or type of the recorder or of the microphone (e.g. omni or unidirectional) is not relevant. I have recorded EVP voices with both but some experimenters recommend the omnidirectional microphone based upon the fact that it can pick up sounds from anywhere in the room or elsewhere within its reach. To this day we do not have a clear idea of how EVP voices are produced; therefore, we cannot connect them to this or that characteristic of the microphone. The microphone can be separate or incorporated into the recorder, as is the case with the small portable digital or tape recorders. If the experimenter prefers to use a detachable microphone, then naturally the microphone should be suitable for the recorder. It can be placed anywhere in the room but the most convenient distance, according to many experimenters, is between 1 and 2 meters from the source of noise. When I started my EVP experimentation one of the first devices I bought was a nice omnidirectional microphone, a fairly expensive Sennheiser that had to be specially ordered at a music shop in Vigo. I was happy to have been able to get it and always used it connected to my good portable Sony tape recorder; but one day a thought crossed my head and I asked the communicators if they preferred the Sennheiser or the microphone incorporated in the little Sony. To my surprise, they replied that they preferred the one in the tape recorder, and from then on I disconnected the Sennheiser and started using the microphone of the tape recorder.

Naturally, if the experimenter can afford it, he or she will prefer to have the most sensitive devices. This is important, not so much for the recording of anomalous voices (something that does not depend on the equipment) but certainly for the quality of the recording itself. However, any devices, without distinction, are in principle adequate. For convenience at the time of playback, the recorder should have a counter and, if possible, a speed control mechanism.

Field Work
There are people who prefer to tape in certain sites, normally connected to interesting historical events or with religious connotations or even in cemeteries. A number of members of the American AA-EVP do this systematic work in places that have the reputation of being haunted.

For many years this procedure was almost a fashion in Spain among the many EVP experimenters. There was also a tendency to search for macabre places where, for instance, a crime had been committed, and tape there. Some ghoulish voices were sometimes made public but although this was a national tendency it was never demonstrated that such places were better for recording voices than neutral places. In my opinion the few chilling voices that were played to satiety in Spanish radio programs, conferences, etc. could have been either the result of a kind of practical joke from the side of the communicators, or they could be the outcome of the capture of remaining psychic energy that, according to the esoteric literature, impregnates the atmosphere when a highly emotional event occurs at a certain place.

Furthermore, ITC operatives, such as the late Sarah Estep, who experimented extensively at home and in field work, reported having recorded some of their customary voices in places of high historical significance such as the Egyptian monuments (Estep, 1988).

In his book, *Voces del Más Allá*, my friend Carlos Fernández refers to a group of researchers in La Coruña that carried out an investigation into the relationship between the recording of anomalous EVP voices and the places where the recordings took place. He quotes some of their main results:

We did not detect any special increment of the phenomenon in function of the experimentation place. Psychophonic voices occur both in the cemetery as well as in the laboratory (Fernández, 2006).

Procedures

The communicators have repeatedly said that the state of mind of the experimenter is of importance for the success of the communication, as previously mentioned several times in the book. It should be the most tranquil and the least anxious as is possible. A few minutes of silence in a state of calm detachment are advisable before the taping session. A few peaceful words or a prayer coming from the heart at the beginning of each recording session will help the state of mind. The experimenter can also ask for the protection and help of a deceased loved one. I believe that, above all, it is important to be authentic and true to oneself. To be as one is, without trying to disguise feelings or thoughts and to accept things as they are, is the best attitude. Our communicators know a lot about us – as a communicator once said to me, 'We know many things' – and they seem to be constantly aware of our intentions and goals.

The reader will have noticed that I have mentioned several times the 'questions' we ask during the experiments. To ask questions is by no means mandatory. Instead of asking questions some people prefer to chat as in a conversation with an invisible interlocutor, while they let the recording device run freely; others will only speak at the beginning of the experiment and then they leave the recording to continue for a few minutes; still others prefer to make and record their own questions and then remain quiet until they make another question. Between each question he or she should allow a lapse of 1 to 2 minutes. This was the method we followed when we started our ITC experiments and it is still the method I prefer.

The questions we ask during the taping session should naturally avoid materialistic issues and requests for predictions about the future. ITC does not serve as an oracle and the communicators do not normally speak about the future. It seems pertinent to quote here a comment received through mediumistic automatic writing on the 28th of July 1939, which belongs to the series of messages received by three generations of the same French family, that I have quoted before, during a period of around fifty years. Apparently, the deceased Jean Winter replied to his mother who had asked him if he could see the future with ' …non je n'ai pas le droit de le lire, et si je le lisais, je n'aurait pas le droit de le dire.' (Literal translation: …no, I have no right to read it, but if I had, I would not be entitled to speak about it.) And he continues, 'Je me contente d'avertissements qui regardent les Êtres en général…' (I confine myself to warnings that concern the Beings in general…) (e. g. Winter, J. and Dampierre, G. 1939).

Our communicators are people who have lived in our world, who have progressed along the path of Life, and for that reason their consciousness has deepened and expanded. They will surely not appreciate being taken for fortune-tellers. I think that it is important to think about them as one thinks of dear friends close to one's heart who are still alive in this world, i.e. with tenderness, care and respect.

Furthermore, the questions we ask, at least when we start

experimenting, should not be worded in a complex way. For instance, if we want to enquire about the development of our ITC work we should not ask, 'What do you think of my method to try to contact your world?' But we should rather say, 'Is my method of trying to contact your world all right for you?' This question can be answered with a single affirmative or negative word. Let us imagine for a moment that the reply is negative. We can then form another question and try to find out why the system is not adequate. Later on, if things progress well, the complexity of the replies we demand from the communicators can grow. It is apparent that the process that allows for instrumental transcommunication contact between the two dimensions demands intimate collaboration and convergence, as I have repeated throughout the book, but it is also very probable that it requires from our interlocutors the difficult job of learning highly sophisticated skills to implement it. After all, they have the active role; they make the communication possible, and that must be an extremely complex task. When, upon my arrival in France, I lived in a hotel in Lyon before I found my own house in that city, I once told my communicators that I was very surprised because they had practically stopped speaking through the DRV, while in my house in Vigo, Spain, they used to speak with me almost every day. To this they replied, 'You do not understand. This is very difficult!'

Recording Schedule

It is highly desirable to establish a regular schedule for the experimentation sessions at least at the beginning, until firm, well-established contacts are achieved. The experimentation may be tried twice or three times a week, always at the same period of the day, preferably in that time between day and night – depending on the season of the year, between 19h00 and 22h00, according to my own experience and considering that I live in southern Europe. However, if the experimenter prefers, he or she can try to ask the communicators if the chosen schedule is appropriate for their communication. The taping sessions should not be too long. No more than 10 or 15 minutes for the recording; that is four or five questions. More time and more questions would mean a more difficult and a longer listening session. When the recording session is over, the experimenter should thank the invisible communicators, with whom contact has hopefully been established, and disconnect the devices.

It is certainly important to decide upon a schedule and to keep to it. If, for instance, you have to travel, take your little recorder or your computer with you and keep to the schedule you have established and/or your communicators have approved. This seems to be an important step and once the contact has been set up stick to it at all costs. At the beginning of my EVP experimentation I unexpectedly needed to go on a trip abroad and told my communicators accordingly. To this they replied, 'Do not lose our contacts!' Fortunately I did not, and anyway, whenever I went away for over 24 hours, I had the habit of always carrying with me a reduced version of my equipment – a little tape recorder and a broadband radio to be used as a source of background noise.

Equipment

I have already spoken about the equipment in the sections above but let us recap and draw up a list:

- Analogue tape recorder, digital recording device or a computer. Any recorder will do, and since presently analogue tape recorders are difficult to find, the experimenter should use a digital recorder or record with a computer. If you use a computer you will need sound processing software that will enable you to record and later listen to the recorded material in the best conditions. I have used 'Sound Forge' almost since the very beginning of my experimentation. I find it very convenient and easy to work with. It is slightly expensive but it is reliable and it allows several sound editing operations that will greatly facilitate your listening work. There are many other good sound editing programs that you will easily find on the Internet – Adobe Audition, WavePad and many others. I have recently downloaded WavePad and found it easy to work with and a good sound editing tool. The use of a digital recorder, even a small pocket one, is convenient because you can download it directly onto your computer and then listen to the recorded material with the aid of the software. In my experience, there is nothing more valuable in the listening stage of ITC research than a computer equipped with the appropriate sound editing software.

- A source of background noise or 'carrier wave'. Practically all kinds of noise can be used as a carrier for the taping of anomalous voices. Some people like the sound of running water, others like to tape using traffic noise as acoustic carrier, others like to record in an open space with the sound of the wind in the foliage – an important piece of advice when using this method is never to tape when the wind is too strong because it will produce undesirable noise in the microphone that will impede anything else from being heard – still others use a dog's ultrasound whistle or a mosquitoes' ultrasound deterrent or the ticking of a clock, etc. The only limit is the experimenter's imagination.

However, there seem to be some acoustic carriers more conducive than others to achieving positive results. As I have indicated, my favorite source of noise is the 'white noise' of radios tuned to the SW band. However, human voices seem to be the vehicle that really facilitates the recording of anomalous voices. Indeed EVP voices appear to be more easily recorded if one uses human voices, such as for example a radio emission in a foreign language, or simply the recording of a conversation between several people, or a proper live conversation as background source of noise. We might speculate that the reason why this happens is perhaps because the communicators use the background noise, the acoustic carrier, to modulate their words and if the carrier is of the same nature to what has to be produced from it (i.e., phonemes), the process would indeed be facilitated. I personally do not advocate this method, used by many with good results, for the simple reason that it is very confusing and it is necessary to be very sharp and careful not to take totally normal voices for anomalous voices, as can very easily happen with the use of a foreign language radio emission. There are many cases of words that have one meaning in one language and the same phonemes have a totally different meaning in another language, in this case in the experimenter's language. Add to this the expectation factor that we discussed before and you will have a false lead! I can never overemphasize that ITC researchers must be extremely careful when considering their own results, and certainly when presenting them publicly. The whole subject will be unnecessarily damaged if an ITC researcher (although innocently because that is his or her honest conviction) presents as anomalous voices what are merely fragments of a radio emission in a foreign language.

In any case, I think that the choice of the carrier should be decided by the experimenters themselves, without importing models. It should be decided on the basis of the quality of the results obtained through some form of acoustic support and not because somebody else uses it with good results. You might try the same carrier and get good results or not; there is no guarantee of any kind that something that works well for one researcher will work as well for somebody else. Nevertheless, one important recommendation is that the background noise used as a carrier for EVP experimentation should not be too loud. It should be relatively soft and of medium amplitude, neither too low nor too loud.

As explained above, the questions should be asked and recorded while the background noise is also being recorded.

Experimentation Log

There can never be too much emphasis on the importance and usefulness of an experimentation log. In this diary, the experimenter should methodically register all possible information concerning the experiment – day and hour, weather conditions, phase of the moon, participants in the session, his or her own mood, and, above all, every single noise produced during the recording session, even the noises produced occasionally by any radio or radios which may be in use. This will avoid a lot of unnecessary concern during the listening work, particularly difficult for the beginner, when he or she hears a recorded noise and wonders if it was naturally or anomalously produced. What does it say? What does it mean? Etc. As I have also explained, at the beginning of ITC experiments it is quite common to find strange noises recorded in your device. These can be, for instance, very loud or not so loud knocks, or something like the sound of little balls bouncing on a hard surface (we had many of these at the beginning), sighs, the sound of breathing, etc.

With your log you will create a valuable document that will enable you, even years later, to have an overall view of the conditions of your experimentation and its results, in order to establish correlations, if any, and learn from them.

The Listening Procedure

This is perhaps the most difficult stage in EVP work, especially at the beginning of the experimentation. You will need all the concentration and motivation you are able to find within yourself, and sit quietly with your headphones on, listening several times to the recording or to a segment of it, particularly where *you think* there may be some little anomalous noise or word. As I said above, sometimes the establishment of the contact is preceded by the occurrence of knocks or clicks on the tape, which were not produced in the room or by the radios. A great deal of attention should be given to these because the voices, which at the beginning may sound almost like a faint whisper, can sometimes be 'pasted' to these knocks or clicks.

I highly recommend that people interested in ITC research listen to their recordings through a pair of good headphones. Here the quality does matter. A pair of low quality headphones may cause more harm than good since they can deform and introduce artifacts in the sound and thus create confusion in the experimenter's mind about the reality, or the content, or both, of the anomalous utterances, if there are any.

However, the most valuable tool to listen to ITC recordings is, undoubtedly, a computer. With it you can easily and rapidly separate the little section of acoustic material you want to listen to, repeat the listening over and over again, equalize it, clean the noise, soften or enhance the sound, etc. If you are minimally apt with computers and can afford it, I strongly advise you to follow this recommendation. With the continuation of the ITC work, you will be grateful that you did. It not only allows a much easier identification of difficult to understand utterances but it also saves the experimenter a lot of time.

I would recommend that you listen to your recordings the next day, preferably in the morning. You will notice that you will be much less tired than immediately after the recording, and you will perceive any little deviation from the normal sounds much more accurately.

Whether you listen to the recordings with a computer or with headphones only, it is always good practice to ask other people, for instance friends or family, to listen to your EVP recordings too and request them to transcribe for you what they hear. This is sound advice that, if put into practice, will give you more confidence and will protect you from being misled by two very important negative factors – expectation and tiredness. Indeed, every time you put a question to your invisible friends you will unconsciously expect to hear a certain type of response. The content of the response you wish to hear will match – and I emphasize the fact that this is a perfectly innocent situation because it will be your unconscious playing games on you – your mental patterns, convictions, ideals, desires and so on. It will also be tailored to your cultural, social and intellectual profile. There is great danger, especially when the utterances are not perfectly clear, that your brain will project the content of the response you would like to hear into the blurred EVP words recorded on your tape. And then you may 'hear' it even though it is not there. The listeners' test, as the practice I referred to above is commonly called, even if done at non-professional level, is a good safeguard against this undesirable occurrence that can jeopardize your work because it may mislead you. If all the listeners of your small group agree with your interpretation (which you do not disclose, prior to them listening, but rather that you have written on a piece of paper) you can be pretty sure that you are on the right path. Once again, each one of them should be requested to write down on a piece of paper what they understand, without informing the others.

The Direct Radio Voices

I do not feel confident to give you much advice concerning the experimentation with the DRV. The reason for this is that there is not much advice that anybody can honestly give you. The DRV can happen or not happen. In my opinion, this is a good sign of the autonomous existence of the communicators and one that contradicts the hypothesis some parapsychologists like to put forward (i.e., the voices being the result of psychokinesis by the experimenter). I am sure that anybody experimenting with ITC would be delighted to get DRV. They are incredibly thrilling because they allow for dialogues, and what else can be more moving or exciting in this world than the possibility of speaking with those we call the deceased who have preceded us in the path of life? Yet to this date, the largest numbers of ITC experimenters do not get DRV and we do not know why this happens. If ITC results were produced by the unconscious psychokinetic action of the experimenter, the DRV would certainly be the preferred target of that action.

There are, however, certain procedures that I can recommend, based upon my own experience. The most important one is to follow the advice given in Luxembourg by the Technician: 'For being able to receive this kind of contacts, perhaps via radio receiver, the regular microphone recordings have to be intensely fostered...' This definitely happened in my case.

The use of radios tuned to the SW band is, in my view, highly desirable because the communicators once said when I asked if the frequency was important, 'To modulate the waves we only need the short waves.' Another possibility is the use of more than one radio even if this is not a requisite for the DRV. From the very beginning, I thought, although I was not aiming at the DRV, that I might facilitate the communicators' work if I provided a rich mixture of radio frequencies for them. I presently have in my studio a number of radios that have been added to throughout the years, according to my communicators' advice and requests. Adolf Homes, the German ITC researcher who was closely monitored by Professor Ernst Senkowski, used five radios, a number very similar to mine.

On the other hand, other researchers, such as Marcello Bacci or my friends, the Portuguese experimenters, Luísa Alcântara and Maria dos Anjos Antunes, use only one radio tuned to the 'white noise' of a SW radio receiver and they also receive DRV. The cases of Luísa Alcântara and Maria dos Anjos Antunes are even more interesting for our present discussion because their communicators also identify themselves as people who speak from Rio do Tempo Station. Both of them started their experimentation after discussing ITC procedures with me, and in both cases they specifically asked to speak with Rio do Tempo. But I restate again that I think it is important that prospective ITC operators always keep in mind that our rules do not apply to this field of research. They should try to find the most adequate methods for them without attempting to import models.

Possible Dangers for the Experimenter

I am frequently asked by interested people to give them advice on the possible dangers that can arise from ITC experimentation. Several authors have warned that such dangers may exist, but it seems to me that these warnings come less from active experimenters and more from theoretical commentators and parapsychologists. My personal opinion is that, generally speaking, these dangers do not exist, provided those who attempt ITC contacts are psychologically stable and well-grounded individuals. Ideally, contacts with the next world should be attempted not just with the aim of exploring the survival hypothesis (although this is a very valid reason), but with the purpose of expanding one's consciousness. The messages conveyed through ITC normally have a high ethical content (Bacci, 1995; Cardoso, 2003, 2005; Locher and Harsch, 1995; Senkowski, 1995). In fact, conveying ethical information seems to be one of the major purposes of the communications. The late Professor Hans Bender, the renowned German parapsychologist that I spoke of in Chapter 2, once said in an ITC communication to leading investigator Adolph Homes:

'People who in experiments to contact us get a negative feeling are not yet ready [for the contacts] on account of their state of consciousness, they should still wait.' (Senkowski ibid, 1995).

Modifying a Radio to Receive 'Broadband' and Function as a Noise Source*

Any radio that receives FM and AM wave bands can be modified to provide audio support for your attempt to receive EVP. It is not necessary that the radio be of good quality. A small portable will do. The modification is simple, and with reasonable care can easily be carried out by the layman.

Before starting work, if the radio is mains powered, it is vital to disconnect the radio from the electricity supply in order to avoid any risk of electric shock. Do not reconnect to the mains supply until all the work is completed and the cover of the radio is correctly in place.

Step 1. Remove the cover of the radio, usually held in place by small screws.

Step 2. Cut the wire connecting the components board to the aerial. The aerial is then inoperative and can be discarded if you wish.

Step 3. Disconnect the variable capacitor responsible for tuning the radio. (For the layman, the variable capacitor in a modern radio is the small transparent plastic box, measuring approximately one and a half centimeters, which is connected to the other components of the tuning circuits.) Cut this connection. As a result, the radio can no longer be tuned to any station, and if turned on would simply emit a continuous noise. (Exceptionally, depending on certain factors such as the place where the radio is being used, for instance in the close proximity of a radio mast, it can still pick up fragments of emissions. However, this is a very rare event.)

Step 4. To complete the modification, the tuning coil should be disabled. (To assist the layman, the tuning coil is a series of fabric covered windings around a central core.) Cut the wires connecting this coil to the component board, severing them as flush with the board as possible.

Step 5.   Refit the cover of the radio, making sure that it is securely screwed back in place before you reconnect the set to the mains electricity supply.

The radio is now ready for use, and when turned on will emit a strong hiss of 'white noise' in both the FM and the AM bands. This noise can be used on its own in your attempt to receive EVP or can be used in conjunction with any other source of random noise (usually a radio tuned between two stations). Make sure that your modified radio is placed at an adequate distance from your microphone (approximately 2 meters).   Adjust the volume of the radio appropriately, bearing in mind that for EVP you only require a moderate level of sound comparable to that received during normal listening.

Grateful thanks are given to Carlos Fernández for providing the technical notes on which this description of modifying a radio for 'broadband' reception is based.

*Improved version of the text published in *ITC Journal 8*, December 2001, p. 16.

Chapter 12

Characteristics of the Voices

Some Interesting Characteristics of the Voices

Most, but not all, ITC voices sound different from normal human voices. This applies especially to the DRV voices. EVP voices, when they are of good acoustic quality, sound more natural and if they are sufficiently loud they are usually clearer and better articulated. We should mention here that there are sounds publicly presented as EVP voices, which probably do not contain one single phoneme. They are merely noise, which sometimes presents a special cadence that the brain interprets as speech as we have seen when we discussed the phenomenon of pareidolia. This is a common occurrence that, to my dismay, I have witnessed many times, even at international conferences and congresses. This is an easy path, mostly directed towards to the bereaved parents of deceased children, who are prone to believe in anything that will alleviate their suffering. However, it is a highly reproachable method that stains the subject and the individuals who practice it. In this book and particularly in this chapter, I shall not consider that type of 'EVP voice'. It is the role of the serious, committed ITC researcher to differentiate between what carries real, objective meaning and what does not.

Many DRV sound muffled, as if uttered from inside a funnel, a tunnel or a box, and sometimes they are also distorted although the degree of distortion may vary. When they do not sound muffled they tend to sound metallic and hard. Nevertheless, this is not a hard and fast rule for we can find many exceptions if we examine the voices received by different successful DRV experimenters and even within the scope of my own DRV. I have recorded clear DRV that could not have sounded more natural while others sound as if they were hammered out by a machine. It is interesting to note that in the famous Luxembourg ITC phenomena, types of additional noises similar to the ones I have recorded were sometimes heard during the reception of the DRV:

> ...during the experiments a low, deep voice tried to make itself heard. For moments we did not receive more than fragments of words and noises that resembled those made by an electric saw...'
>
> (Locher and Harsch, 1995, p. 116)

Indeed, based on my own experience, the similarity to an electric saw could not have been more appropriate to characterize sounds that I have recorded in the course of some DRV contacts.

The special singing rhythm that we often find in EVP voices, frequently mentioned in the specialized literature, occasionally happens in some DRV also, although it cannot be considered a distinctive feature of the latter.

Another common aspect of many anomalous voices (EVP and DRV) is an increase in speed in comparison to normal human voices. Nevertheless, the increase in the speed of the speech is not uniform. It can vary from slightly faster to a lot faster. And, although a rarer event, some voices can also be comparatively slower than normal human voices. It is also interesting to note that during the same communication an anomalous voice can suddenly change its rhythm and/or speed. In my view the question is: what is behind these special features? Why do they happen? Are the communicators conscious of them? I think that perhaps they are (or it may be more accurate to say that sometimes they are) because they have made remarks that allow me to make such an affirmation. Sometimes through DRV, for instance, 'Muito comprimidas as vozes,' (the voices are very compressed). Sometimes recorded as an EVP, 'Há marcado ruído,' (there is a lot of noise). Their observations were invariably pertinent to the actual situation of the contact taking place.

An alleged characteristic of the EVP voices (I have seen it attributed to some DRV, also) is based upon the theory that sometimes the voices can be reversed (i.e. played backwards) and they will carry a different meaning from when they are played in the normal direction. They are the so-called 'reversed voices'. They are often presented as an example of the 'paranormality' of electronic voices. Although I have recorded a few of those too, I would not guarantee that they are real reversed anomalous voices. Sometimes reversed voices do carry a certain meaning to the ear because they are speech played backwards, but again there is the risk that it is the brain projecting meaning into blurred and abstruse vocalizations through the phenomenon of pareidolia. We should be aware of this possibility before drawing definitive conclusions. As it is the case for anomalous voices in general, the reversed anomalous voices should only be considered acceptable if their intelligibility is good (See example on the CD).

An important piece of advice when we speak about the voices, or even about ITC research in general, is to avoid generalizations. If we make definite statements about ITC phenomena we will certainly make mistakes. I often employ the word 'sometimes' when I speak of psychophonic events because, in my opinion, this is an important precaution. To my knowledge, there have always been exceptions to any generalization about Instrumental Transcommunication research and its results.

There is a good deal of published material that attempts to determine the characteristics of EVP voices. My recommendation to the reader is that none of it should be taken as a definition of the voices because definitions do not apply in this field. Let us see, for example, the length attributed to EVP voices which is normally of three to four words not exceeding between 1.50 sec. to 1.75 seconds (MacRae, 1984). One of the most perfect (from the point of view of language and clarity) EVP voices that I recorded is: 'Claro que não tem nada que ver, a ilusão que temos nós, eles não me podem ouvir tem de ser através do mar. (Of course it has nothing to do with it [speaking loudly or lowly], the same illusion that we have, they cannot hear me it has to be through the sea). Discussed in previous chapters, this has two main characteristics – it by far exceeds the number of words attributed to EVP and it reaches slightly over six seconds of speech, more than tripling the time duration attributed to those messages. Furthermore, the feminine voice, although perhaps not perfectly identical, is very similar to my own voice. I even have the impression that this anomalous voice of enigmatic content has replaced my own voice (i.e., perhaps it was constructed with the phonemes of the sentence that I uttered), which obviously consisted of different words (naturally I cannot recall the content of everything I said on that extraordinary evening of March 29, 1998). If, as I suspect, this was the case, regrettably my own words no longer exist on that particular segment of the tape, but my voice is everywhere throughout this very long DRV contact that lasted for over two hours and thirty minutes and was witnessed by my friend Carlos Fernández from the very beginning. I aim to have this voice analyzed at the highest technical-scientific level for comparison with my own voice.

Discussing this rather common and disconcerting event with the knowledgeable Ernst Senkowski, he wrote back to me,

The similarity – in my view – could well be the result of the fact that the original trans-message is mediated by the experimenter as a telepathic receiver and the form of the outcome contains parts of his/her structure. I had an example in which a clear EVP/VOT said, '*Gott ist wirklich da* (*God is really there*).' It is a voice similar to my own voice but what it says is against my convictions (Senkowski 2009, personal correspondence).

Another exceptional example again comes from Senkowski who says:

The longest EVP sentence – 36 syllables – that I ever taped runs unequivocally understandable: *'Wir müssen jetzt das Pulverfaß nehmen und per Funk fragen Ernst Otto Senkowski, ob Sie mal Ski Fahren gehen mit Ihrer Tochter Regina'*. (We must now take the powder barrel and by wireless ask Ernst Otto Senkowski whether you [singular] will some time go skiing with your daughter Regina.) The duration of this sentence is of around 10 seconds.

Senkowski also reports on messages from his wife Adelheid:

There have been several EVP/VOT contacts with *Adelheid* after I called her. The best was the one I mentioned: Sitting beside the switched-on radio I said: 'Hast du eine Mitteilung für mich, liebe Adelheid?' (Have you a message for me, dear Adelheid?) And a clear female voice without noisy background immediately answered word by word *'Hallo - hier - Adelheid – bitte.'* (Hello - here - Adelheid – please.) I did not hear it directly from the loudspeaker in spite of the fact that it was a <u>loud</u> voice on the tape (EVP voice) (Senkowski, 2009 personal correspondence).

The Use of Several Languages

A very interesting feature of my own DRV, especially in the past, is that they sometimes included a few words in Spanish scattered here and there in the middle of the Portuguese speech. A good example of this happened when, one day, I suddenly slowed down my own articulation of the words, while talking to my invisible partners, and immediately a feminine voice introduced very clearly, 'Porque fala tão (Portuguese) despacio (Spanish)?' (Why are you speaking so slowly?) This DRV is included in the CD.

Equally interesting is the use of the Spanish word 'perro' (dog) and in one instance the use of 'dog' in English, instead of the

Portuguese word 'cão'. The word 'cão' has a much muffled sound because of the nasal diphthong. Will this be the reason for the systematic use of 'Perro'? It is possible but again we cannot be sure. For the time being, only the communicators know the reason.

However, as I said above, in my case, the use of Spanish words happened mostly at the beginning of the DRV – it markedly happened with the very first direct radio voice that I tend to attribute to Carlos de Almeida because the masculine voice sounds very much like the voice of the communicator who later identified himself as Carlos de Almeida. It occasionally happened in France where I resided from the beginning of the year 2000. In that country the voices mixed a couple of words in Spanish here and there but I recall none in French. It has not happened in Spain where I have lived again since my return from France in 2004. The communicators now speak mostly in Portuguese, unless they are especially required to do otherwise by foreign observers (as it happened a few times with Professor David Fontana), or if a guest of a different nationality is present at the recording session, although, in those cases, they have a tendency to intersperse words in Portuguese in their speech.

This is what happened on 18th of August 1998, when I received the visit of an ITC investigator who spoke in English with me, although this is not his native language. The communicator, who identified himself right at the beginning of the DRV contact as Homero, said, among other things, in Portuguese, 'Homero, Homero, Homero. This is Rio de todo. This is Rio de todos. This is Rio do Tempo!' (Homero, Homero, Homero. This is the river of the whole. This is the river of all. This is Rio do Tempo!) On the same occasion, when I asked the communicators if they could 'leave an EVP message for our guest', a beautifully loud and clear feminine voice appeared recorded on the tape saying in Portuguese and Italian 'Sei parlare!' (I know how to speak.) (See CD). Interestingly, a voice recorded by Raudive, the transcript of which I only discovered in *Breakthrough,* page 42, a few weeks ago, uses exactly the same words. In this case, a communicator, apparently his own deceased brother, Alex, tells him 'Ja prūtu sprechen' (translation: I know how to speak).

Some other EVP voices, which I recorded, also included words in languages other than Portuguese, as for example the beautiful, 'Natal, un beso for Nina.' Translation: Christmas (Portuguese), a kiss (Spanish) for (English) and Nina is the name of one of my little dogs that used to remain with me in my studio during my ITC experimentation. I recall another occasion when a communicator, who identified herself as Joan Colbert in reply to my question, 'Who is speaking', responded to me mostly in perfect Portuguese, intermingled with a couple of words in English, and continued speaking in English for some time, apparently to somebody in her world.

The multi-language use has already been referred to extensively by Friedrich Jürgenson and Konstantin Raudive, both of whom were accomplished polyglots. The DRV received by Marcello Bacci at his Psychophonic Center at Grosseto usually include words in a number of other languages besides Italian, although Bacci himself is not proficient in those languages (e.g. ITC Journal 2005, nº 21). However, on those occasions, there are normally people amongst the assistants at the center who will understand the meaning of the communicators' words. This is what happened to me on one of the occasions that I was there. The communicators spoke with me in Portuguese interspersed with a number of Spanish words, although I insisted with them to address me in Portuguese only. It was on this very occasion that one of the voices forwarded what I consider a remarkable explanation, to which I have given great thought.

While speaking to the voices, at a certain point I said: 'AC - Obrigada por falar comigo, pode falar comigo em Português por favor?' (Thank you for speaking with me, can you speak with me in Portuguese, please?) And I continued: 'AC .... desculpe, mas pode falar em Português, por favor? (Sorry, but can you speak in Portuguese, please?)

Communicator: '...lo **que isto é** increíble.' (...But this is incredible.) 'AC – É increíble? Obrigada por tentar falar comigo em Português.' (It's incredible? Thanks for trying to speak with me in Portuguese.)

'C – Porque el mundo **é grande**, tenga en cuenta que **as línguas** son tantas, más me dicen con las ondas de la radio arriva todo, y escuchando, me dicen que cambia **à sua língua.'** *(Spanish, Portuguese and one Italian word 'arriva'. Note: the words that are Portuguese only, not common to Spanish, are in bold.)* (Because the world is big, take into consideration that there are so many languages. Moreover, I am told that with the radio waves everything arrives, and by listening, I am told that it changes into your language) (The full text is published in ITC Journal Nº 25, April 2006).

The sentence that particularly puzzles me in this remarkable interchange, the content of which should be explored in depth, is the second part: '… más me dicen con las ondas de la radio arriva todo, y escuchando me dicen que cambia à sua lingua.' (…Moreover I am told that with the radio waves everything arrives and, by listening, I am told that it changes into your language.) In my opinion, there is here an important reference by the communicator to the role of the experimenter (and/or participants/assistants) as the agent responsible for the transformation of the signal into meaning (language). Furthermore, it clearly states that the signal 'arrives with the radio waves'. These are fundamental but still obscure points in the extraordinary field of ITC research, which should be investigated with the modern tools of science.

The Odd Syntax of Many ITC Sentences
Readers have certainly realized throughout the book – even if the translation cannot properly reflect all the grammar oddities,

although I have kept it as literal as possible – that many of the voices I have quoted use a very unusual sentence structure. A good example to illustrate this point is, for instance, the important communication that informs us that the time of death is predetermined. The voice said, among other things, 'Anabela, the time is predetermined. You can 'make the step and the commitment'…' Although the meaning of the metaphor, 'make the step and the commitment', is obvious (you can be absolutely sure of it), a Portuguese speaker would never use such words to put that information across. What is more, I dare to affirm that many Portuguese speakers will have difficulty in understanding it.

Konstantin Raudive also spoke about the syntax peculiarities of most of his voices, as did Hildegard Schäfer and almost all other researchers. In general, they assumed that the communicators tried to express their thoughts and feelings with a maximum of time/energy saving; therefore, using language in a very synthetic, but meaningful way. This appears to be a good conjecture but the truth is that, to this date, we do not know for sure what is implied in the production of the voices.

The use of notions such as time and energy is quite awkward in relation to voices which declare that they come from 'another dimension beyond time', as communicators from Rio do Tempo have said to me. Perhaps we should not even mention such concepts but we, researchers, have no other way of conveying our impressions to our readers and other people interested in the fascinating world of Instrumental Transcommunication.

Jürgenson puts it that:

The language of the dead is the unvarnished pictorial language of the subconscious. Free of any compromises whether these may be caused by false politeness, stylist prettiness or moral concerns of any kind, 'the language of the dead' transmits directly the truth of the heart.

I fully endorse his remark, but I also think that good, intelligent and specialized research is urgently needed in order to try and understand the process a little further.

Are ITC voices similar to the voices of the people they are supposed to belong to?

Another problematic issue is the question of whether the voices are similar or otherwise to the voices of the people they are supposed to belong to when they lived on Earth.

One of my contacts – I tend to think it was Joan Colbert because the voice sounded very similar to the feminine voice that spoke with me many times and identified herself as Joan Colbert's – answered my question, 'Can you tell me how do you produce your voices?' through DRV with, 'Damos-lhe a certeza que mascaramos, fazem-nos um sonograma.' (You can be sure that we masquerade. They do us a sonogram.) See CD.

And the deceased Konstantin Raudive is reported as saying in Luxembourg, '..... it was said that the voices were not perfectly the same. Friends, the paranormal cannot be repeated,' (Schäfer ibid, p. 106). However, Friedrich Jürgenson reports that he could often recognize the voices of individuals whom he knew well from their particular timbre and speech expressions. Another remarkable example is forwarded by Professor Senkowski, himself an accomplished ITC experimenter and researcher, who informed me through personal correspondence, 'I taped the nearly original voice of my father addressing me with my two forenames and my nickname in his East-Prussian dialect, on Jan. 14, 1977. He said on tape: *'Ernst-Ottchen, mein lieber Pumuckel.'* *(Ernst-Ottchen, my dear pumuckel.)* And Senkowski added, 'Ottchen is a diminutive of Otto, my second forename. Father used to call me so when I was a little boy. Pumuckel is a nickname familiar in the Eastern parts of Europe representing a dwarf who played all sorts of jokes.' Senkowski went on to say, 'The voice that I found in replaying the tape was absolutely spontaneous and impressed me strongly emotionally. Indeed I could not contain my tears. I am absolutely sure that I did not even think of my father or any other relation while I was experimenting.'

In Théo Locher and Maggy Harsch's book, it is reported that

...the Technician assured Maggy that they would try to synthesize the voice of this woman [Margret Mackes, a friend of Maggy Harsch] as closely as possible. In fact, her husband immediately recognized her voice. On other occasions, says Mrs. Harsch, the voices sounded different from the voices of the people they were supposed to belong to, while alive. [The contacts were through DRV.]

From their side, Scott Rogo and Bayless say on page 136 of their book that I mentioned in previous chapters:

...We collected no fewer than three instances of these record player voices, which constitute even further evidence that the dead can communicate with the living by producing 'prints' of their own terrestrial voices over electrical equipment.

Indeed, the issue of the voices (especially the DRV) sounding either different or similar to the voices of the human personalities they are supposed to belong to is very intriguing, but I think that it could also be related to the 'very, very difficult' work required by the communications, as Carlos de Almeida and others from Rio do Tempo Station have emphasized on numerous occasions. If, as it seems, the radio proper is used as the vehicle for the transmission or production of the voices – a point which, to my knowledge, has not yet been clarified – maybe the apparatus itself plays a role in this as well.

Related to the difficulties involved in the making of the voices must be the incidents that I reported more extensively about in

Chapter 10. Rio do Tempo communicators often request me to leave the radios on night and day for several days at a time, and their voices can be heard repeating loudly: 'We are all dead..., Rio do Tempo... We are the dead... We are the dead from Tempo, Aunt, Father, November, etc.' (Translation from the Portuguese original). They also repeat, 'Alpha, beta' and many other words that cannot be properly understood. Their repetitions can be heard night and day interspersed with long periods of silence. Sometimes the communicators' voices are clear, often they are blurred and distorted, and every now and then they produce a tremendous echo and display many other odd characteristics. 'We are working. We cannot speak with you today,' they tell me when I complain that they are not speaking to me. There is one more remarkable parallel to this situation in Gabriela Alvisi's book, *Le Voci dei Viventi di Ieri* (1976). In it she describes what she qualifies as 'diction exercises' carried out by her deceased daughter who told her, 'Mama, I am learning!' when she questioned her about the weakness of her and other communicators' voices.

However, as said above, it seems that EVP voices in general tend to be more similar to the voices of the people they are supposed to belong to. In my own experiments this was confirmed by a very moving experience. While recording a DRV communication, the very short but loud and clear word, 'João,' (John in English) appeared recorded on the tape as an EVP. When I listened to it, I thought that it might have to do with Juan, Lola's eighteen-year-old deceased son. That same night I called Lola on the telephone and without previous warning put the tape recorder near the telephone mouthpiece and played that bit. From the other side of the line she shouted, 'How do you have my son's voice there?' The audio sample was submitted to voice-print analysis in comparison with the voice of the boy reciting Garcia Lorca when he was fourteen, but as the report says,

Unfortunately, due to the scarcity of the available evidence – the analysis was based upon only a single EVP word – it was impossible to identify the voice with the help of the objective parametrical methods that would give us a higher level of reliability. Nevertheless, there is enough data to allow us to conclude that the EVP voice can be considered compatible with the living voice, that is to say it is not dissimilar, as the tracks of the formants F4 and F5, which mainly characterize the individual features of the speaker, for the two voices show a similarity of 74%. (Gullà 2005)

The Anomalous Electronic Voices Can Be Similar to the Experimenter's Own Voice

One of the most puzzling features of the EVP voices is the fact that they sometimes – once again the process is not consistent – resemble the experimenter's own voice or, more rarely, the voice of another person present in the room. We could speculate that, as an outcome of resonance, the communicators telepathically access the experimenter's (and/or participants') language patterns and use them in the construction of the words that will convey their ideas through a process still unknown to us.

I have discussed this point with Professor Senkowski and with other researchers, and nobody had a straightforward explanation for this odd event. Ernst Senkowski described it as 'structural resonance', clarifying that the expression could be understood as resonance of the whole of the consciousness content (or mind-field) between the experimenter on Earth and the transcendental communicator(s).

As would be expected, the defenders of the psychokinetic hypothesis use this incident as 'proof' to substantiate their theories but this is far from proving anything. In fact, in some cases the voices can, as we saw above, be similar to the experimenter's voice but they do not sound perfectly identical (to the ear). As far as I know, no technical forensic analyses of the anomalous voices versus the experimenters' voices have been made for comparison, and they are urgently needed. I will add that to manage to get a reliable, reputable Acoustics Research Institute to perform such analyses is a feat in itself and, more often than not, an unachievable goal. Such tests are not only very costly but, more decisive is the fact that, as a general rule, the scientists who work in prestigious acoustics institutions, once they are told the presumed origin of the audio samples sent for their examination, will return them without having performed any technical verification. Most of them will not even bother to forward a polite excuse.

As mentioned, the situation that we are discussing – the resemblance between the anomalous voices and the experimenter's own voice – can happen in EVP voices but, as far as I know, not in the DR voices. Moreover, I have recorded DRV that say disconcerting things such as, 'Vai buscar uma voz.' (Go and get a voice.) Or 'Traz uma voz.' (Bring a voice.) This is another occurrence that greatly puzzles me and for which, to this date, I have found no explanation. I once recorded a very clear feminine DRV that suddenly said, 'Ai que se vai a minha voz! (Oh, my voice is going!) And we should again enquire: what accounts for this so bewildering phenomenon – i.e. as a general rule the radio voices do not resemble the human experimenters' or participants' voices while the EVP can strongly resemble the latter? Could it be related to the 'sonograma' mentioned by the Technician and Rio do Tempo in the context of the DRV? As we saw before, it is common knowledge that the most complex contacts, such as the DRV, need the intermediation of a special Center or Station, and seemingly require the 'sonogram' of the deceased person's voice to get across through a radio. Besides, DRV can sound strangely similar to each other. This is particularly true for those voices that can be heard talking to each other incessantly but it is also a proposition that should not be generalized. Carlos de Almeida's voice, for instance, was undoubtedly different from other DRV.

EVP voices are normally much shorter and their production/transmission process must be different. However, from our point of view, since we ignore practically all the factors involved in the process, this simple verification does not contribute much to advance our understanding of it, either. It only confirms that we know so very little about the whole subject (formation and transmission of the voices) and that much more needs to be investigated.

Is the content of the messages conveyed by the voices supervised by a higher power?

One of the longest DRV communications that I received from Carlos de Almeida happened on September 2, 1998 and it lasted for over two and a half hours. It consisted of an uninterrupted exchange of questions (from my side) and replies (from his side), some of which took over three minutes of uninterrupted speech, in an amazing down pouring of information from what appears to be a higher level of existence. Nevertheless, to my great dismay, most of his speech could not be properly deciphered because, although it sounded very loud and apparently articulate to direct hearing, upon listening to it attentively, with the purpose of apprehending the full information it contained, it became obvious that most of the content could not be under-stood. To the ear, his voice (it was very similar to the voice that identified itself many times before as belonging to Carlos de Almeida although less modulated) sounded as if projected from a machine with a lid at the opening from where the sound came from. It consisted of clearly defined, abrupt impulses that did not blend with each other. On this issue, remarked Senkowski, 'We have been told that they send short pulses containing long contents of which we receive only a very limited part,' (Senkowski, 2009, personal correspondence.)

I took a sample of this long recording to a local sound design shop and was told by them that there were pieces of words missing in the speech which obviously could not be reconstructed because the problem was not the distortion of the voice; the real problem was that fragments of speech were missing in almost all the words. The identification of Rio do Tempo, some phrases such as 'nós somos todos mortos' (we are all dead), 'vai tardar a ponte' (the bridge will take some time) etc. could be understood but most of it could not.

Speaking about the bridge, it seems pertinent to confirm that it was only on the 15th of March 1999 that Carlos de Almeida announced, 'Já pus a ponte.' (I have already placed the bridge.) See CD. During this communication, he also jokingly said to me (after I intruded into what appeared to be their conversation in order to draw attention to myself), 'Eu desço, você não resiste!' ([If] I come down [to Earth] you will be unable to resist me!) What could be a better example of the touching human quality of our dear invisible partners?

I still hope that one day innovative technology may be able to solve the problem of that particular communication of September 2, 1998 because in that beautifully warm late afternoon, sitting on the floor of my studio with tears coming down my face, I asked my interlocutor of another world a lot of metaphysical questions that I consider of utmost interest to us, humans. Carlos de Almeida's replies may be fundamental for our understanding of life and its ways.

The next day, on September 3, Carlos de Almeida spoke again – that was the day when he said, 'É p'ra essa gente humilde, é convocar o amor, panaceia do mundo seria bonito, não é?' (It is for humble people. It is to call upon love, [the] panacea of the world. It would be beautiful, would it not?) One of the sentences that could also be understood was the comment I mentioned above, 'Muito comprimidas as vozes.' This could be related to the communication of the previous day and to the way the voices sounded on those two occasions. It seems to correspond also to

Senkowski's explanation '...they send short pulses containing long contents of which we receive only a very limited part.' Although this DR voice of September 3rd still sounded like a bullet projected from a partially blocked machine, it was more modulated than the evening before.

I sometimes wonder if, given the delicate nature of the issues I inquired about on September 2, 1998, a higher power intervened to prevent us from getting the information I was so keen on obtaining. We should not forget that, as other researchers and I have reported elsewhere, the communicators themselves have repeatedly informed us that they are not allowed to reply to certain questions. (I suppose that permission must, amongst other factors, depend on the subject, too.) And furthermore, that often they are not allowed to communicate at all. This information has been received on Earth at least since Dr. Raudive's contacts. For instance, Hildegard Schäfer, on page 267 of her book (1993), says that on one occasion she asked the communicators, 'Can you communicate [with us]?' and the voice replied, 'It is allowed now and then.'

We Seem to Be Able to Hear Conversations from Another Dimension

This is a fairly frequent occurrence that has been identified from the very beginning of the electronic voices (Jürgenson, 1967; Alvisi, 1983; Schäfer, 1993, among others) and one that puzzles me a lot – how can we hear a flowing, effortless conversation carried out among themselves by communicators who say that they speak from another dimension? At times they can even be heard making surprising comments to each other such as, 'It is Anabela asking about the making of the voices again,' or similar comments about other issues and then, without a pause, we can hear them uninterruptedly talking to each other again. If we are lucky, there is sometimes what seems to be a temporary halt in their animated conversation and they will briefly reply to us to immediately continue talking to each other. Usually, when this strange situation happens, the voices sound more natural and often are not distorted, but they can also appear and disappear suddenly.

David Scott Rogo and Raymond Bayless, during their early exploration of the telephone calls attributed to the dead, also found that 'several voices' could be heard speaking all at the same time, during some of the anomalous telephone calls compiled in their book (Scott Rogo and Bayless, 1979).

What exactly do we hear – the communicators' thoughts or their words deliberately produced through an act of volition? It seems to me that the former is more likely to be true but we cannot be sure. Or maybe both are correct – sometimes we hear their unhampered thoughts, and other times we hear their thoughts deliberately and with great difficulty transformed into words specifically addressed to us.

If this aspect of the communication process is true (i.e. that sometimes we can, under given conditions, unbeknown to us, hear the communicators' thoughts), it could also explain the odd sentence structure often found in ITC voices, a characteristic that has been a topic of discussion in almost every book on ITC research. I contemplate the fact that 'thought' could have a different grammar expression from formal, deliberate speech.

Professor Senkowski called the voices the 'materialized thoughts' of the communicators (Holbe, 1987, 1989). I find this to be a very good description because some ten years before I read Senkowski's statement, which I only found recently, I already had the impression that I could hear the communicators' thoughts.

Does the 'opening of a door' between dimensions happen in ITC?

I believe that we can still make another conjecture – the likelihood that such occurrences illustrate an extraordinary event – the momentary opening of a door between two dimensions (or worlds if we prefer the term) that allows us to briefly peep into the next level of life. A good model to consider is Ervin Laszlo's proposition (Laszlo, 2008), one that coincides, at least partially, with what I will explore next.

One very important feature of the extraordinary occasions when we can hear the communicators' conversations is that, when they reply to us in the middle of the long chats amongst themselves, their speech sounds as effortless and fluid as their voices talking to each other. Naturally, I report on my own contacts.

One of my EVP voices is a good example of what I am suggesting, because the loud bang of a door closing, which was not produced in my studio or in my house, appeared clearly recorded on one of my experimental tapes. On that particular evening, I had fervently requested the communicators to convey a message to my 'dear father'. After I pronounced the last words, a guttural, loud, imposing masculine voice can be heard in the recording saying slowly, 'O Pai vive!' (The father lives!) This is followed by the sound of heavy steps (not produced in the recording environment or elsewhere outside or inside the house) and after those, the loud bang of a door firmly closing can be heard in the tape with impressive clarity.

Will the 'opening of a door' be responsible for the good quality of the voices? Will it be that when the 'opening' does not or cannot occur the voices sound distorted and muffled, and only some words can be understood here and there? If this is the case, what prompts the 'opening of the door'? As other researchers, I believe that the so-called resonance, or affinity, between the communicators and the experimenter(s) on Earth plays an important role in the process as we discussed in Chapter 10, but I also think that it is not the one and only. However, the important question is: in which way can we, experimenters on Earth, help with the 'opening of the door'? This is a main concern that, to date, has not been definitely solved, and in my opinion we should endeavor to realize this path.

In *The Road to Immortality*, there is another passage of the communications attributed to the deceased Frederic Myers that I find relevant in this context. As a matter of fact, the representation of the next levels of life described in the book appears convincingly coincident to what contemporary survival research through electronic media tells us. Speaking about the *Plane of Colour*, that I mentioned in previous chapters, says Myers:

In this many-coloured region the form vibrates with extreme intensity, for now mind expresses itself more directly in form: so that we can hear the thoughts of other souls. At first only one at a time may break upon that hearing. But after a while we become sensible of the fact that we may hear the thoughts of several souls, each apart and distinct from the other. (p. 57).

The parallel is self-evident. Hence, I believe that we could appropriately propose that, on certain occasions, when we can hear the communicators speaking among themselves, we are in touch with still another level of existence, a level 'above' the next level from where we normally receive our ITC communications. It is pure speculation, but it is perhaps a likely one.

Conclusion

I reiterate that a thorough examination of the anomalous electronic voices at the highest scientific, technical and psychological levels is a top priority that remains to be carried out. I speak of the technical-scientific voice-print tests developed by modern computer science, currently in use in other domains of human activity, namely in judicial cases. In Bologna, Italy, Il Laboratorio, an institution directed by Dr. Enrico Marabini, dedicated to the evaluation of anomalous phenomena through the use of modern tools, as mentioned in chapter 2, is trying to pursue the path launched by distinguished Italian researchers, namely Dr. Renato Orso, many years ago (Presi, 1990, 2009). A lot more work needs to be systematically done in this area. But there are prerequisites that must be complied with in order to validate this type of test, which can be of utmost interest for the advancement of our field of investigation. Firstly, the individuals involved – ITC researchers and technicians – must be people of irreproachable reputation and the methods of evaluation, implemented under carefully controlled conditions, must be the same as those that the Courts of Justice stipulate for judicial cases.

Apparently, the scientific examination of the objective evidence provided by ITC results seems to be an easy goal to achieve but, in reality, as I hinted above, it is far from being so, because the obsolete prejudices of the scientific community on the whole play a decisive role in this scope. Unfortunately, any high profile technician or scientist will, in general, not only refuse to examine the evidence but also refuse to supervise the reception at origin of the voices to be analyzed, another indispensable requisite. I am not sure if the responsibility of this regrettable attitude lies on the scientists' own mental models or if it lies on the capitalist-materialistic system that prevails in the world. Science funding resources, overall, originate in major corporations and their view is bound to play a decisive role in the scientific community's attitude. I believe that both conditions combine to create the present status quo that is primarily responsible for the antagonistic attitude on the part of scientists that we face in this area.

Obviously, a shifting in the prevalent paradigm is urgently needed. And we, ITC researchers and experimenters, should strive to achieve an ambitious goal – the recognition by science of the possibility of communication with another dimension of reality. When and if this goal is achieved, a paradigm shift will naturally occur. Nothing could be more timely and valuable.

Chapter 13

The Future

Alternative Explanations?

Many speculative theories have been published on the possibility that anomalous electronic voices originate with extraterrestrial intelligence. In fact, among a number of parapsychologists in Spain, for example, this is a relatively common assumption.

In my opinion several factors have conspired to give rise to this idea. The first is that, as discussed in an earlier chapter, to the physical senses of the living, death appears to be final. It is, thus, very difficult for the majority of people, even those from whom we would expect a more enlightened attitude as they are familiar with the existence of subtle extrasensory perceptions, to equate the concept of an objectively observable dead body with that of an invisible surviving non-physical consciousness. Central to their difficulty is the deeply rooted conviction that the visible is all there is, so influenced are they with the exclusively materialistic conception of life that has become so deeply rooted in Western culture.

The second relevant factor is that there are, in fact, many reported incidents in the literature suggestive of the direct intervention in our world of alien entities. The truth of this cannot and should not be denied. I am not particularly conversant with this literature myself, but its existence is common knowledge for most of those interested in psychic matters. Of course some commentators (including, in fact, Carl Jung himself) suggest that UFOs and related phenomena are not material at all but represent psychic experiences on the part of observers. This suggestion may of course be correct, but even if this is the case, this may still leave some phenomena that are more readily explained in physical terms.

Taken together, these two factors help account for attempts to link ITC voices to aliens rather than to the deceased. The theory seems to be that alien intelligences telepathically scan us and our world and use the knowledge thus gained to construct their anomalous voices. This theory should not be too readily discarded, since we have no way of knowing if indeed there are, in the Universe or Universes, entities capable of such impressive feats. Much may depend on the level of their evolutionary development, and we are in no position to know what this level may be, since we are of course limited by our own finite understanding.

However, if we take the extraterrestrial hypothesis seriously, I think several questions immediately come to mind – why would the aliens tell us they are deceased people? What would be their purpose in doing so? Some researchers with whom I have exchanged ideas on this subject argue that they may do so in order to gain our confidence, but my reply is, once again, what would be their purpose for doing so? And in view of the high ethical teachings behind many ITC communications, why would they wish, nevertheless, to deceive us in this way? If indeed the intention of ITC communicators is to bring about a generalized expansion of human consciousness and eventually a paradigm shift, why and in what way would this be in the interest of alien entities? These are all questions that need to be answered. In addition, we should also take into consideration that:

- ITC communicators insist repeatedly that they are the deceased. Furthermore, they tell us that although there are indeed extraterrestrials in their sphere of life, the individuals concerned have also passed through the hardships of a physical existence in other worlds.

- We already possess a great deal of evidence accumulated throughout the centuries by a variety of other means, such as mediumship and others, indicating that death is not final and that the deceased do communicate with the living.

With these thoughts in my mind, I once asked Rio do Tempo why is there such a widespread belief in favor of the extraterrestrial hypothesis in regard to ITC communications? To this they responded with what was, for me, a completely unexpected answer: 'São grupos negativos no nosso mundo que não querem que os humanos saibam que a vida continua.' (It is negative groups in our world that do not want humans to know that life continues.) Furthermore, communicators also tell us that positive and negative influences from their world constantly and extensively permeate our world. If we take this information seriously, as I think we should do, the explanation that ITC voices indeed originate with the deceased rather than with extraterrestrials appears convincing.

The Future

In view of what we have discussed in previous chapters, I strongly believe that any assumptions on the future of ITC are premature and out of place. The so far unexplained messages that have reached humanity throughout the centuries have one main point in common – they purport to originate in another level of reality and, as a rule, their authors claim to be 'the dead'.

Due to the unscrupulous behavior of those who claim to have mediumistic gifts but who have resorted to trickery or deceit, much of the evidence advanced in favor of survival is very suspect, and has inevitably invited the ridicule of the scientific community. This point was made forcefully over a century ago by the late Hereward Carrington, one of the foremost researchers into mediumship, who was an expert in detecting fraud or

215

trickery when it occurred (Carrington, 1907). This situation has led scientists to reject or overlook even genuine evidence for survival, in spite of its quality. The arrogance and unfairness of this attitude in regard to reality, driven primarily by influential sections of the scientific community, have had the result of seriously hindering the proper examination, analysis and study of the subject.

The attitude of dismissal in the face of the evidence for survival accumulated throughout the centuries (e.g. Fontana, 2005) has not only persisted but has become even more apparent in our present age of rampant materialism and intellectual reductionism, much of which stems from the thinking of leading scientists. Thinking that is based on Newtonian physics rather than upon what Ervin Laszlo calls the 'new scientific reality,' which he himself explores so effectively in his many publications (most recently Laszlo, 2008).

Instrumental Transcommunication, for the first time in history, offers the possibility of repeatable experiments highly indicative of the survival of physical death of all forms of consciousness. At present, although ITC phenomena cannot always be received on demand, it is, nevertheless, clear that they repeat themselves frequently all over the world under conditions that include a range of similar characteristics. By their nature, ITC results can be scientifically analyzed, measured, assessed etc. by means of the very Newtonian procedures so much to the liking of the majority of the scientific community and of modern-day society in general. Sadly, the scientific community at large refuses to look at, and even less to examine, the evidence provided by ITC results and in consequence frustrates the communicators' expressed purpose, which is to submit the objective, clear electronic ITC results to proper scientific scrutiny and evaluation.

A scientific verdict on the possibility of survival is, in fact, the only way of shaking the materialistic mindset of the billions of humans now inhabiting the Earth, and of contributing decisively to a paradigm shift.

The discovery and development of ITC contacts by our invisible friends seem to constitute another generous objective of their endeavors, which is to contribute to this paradigm shift in our consciousness, and thus to help significantly in our own development as a species. If ever accomplished, this shift would not only help humans grow through the expansion of their consciousness, it would help all other species and the Planet as a whole, because, as a result of Providence or of evolution or of a combination of both, the Planet is actually at the mercy of our present barbaric human ways.

If and when the 'doors of perception were cleansed' – as the visionary poet William Blake so admirably puts it – 'everything would appear to man as it is, infinite.' This cleansing of human perception, if ever attained, might also involve an expansion of the consciousness of other species besides our own. A range of factors might help to lead to this, the main one being that it is through peace, respect and harmony that all living beings in their different degrees of awareness can have the conditions in which to develop positively, already in our world. I have mentioned a quotation from Rio do Tempo elsewhere in the book and it seems appropriate to repeat it here, namely the reply they gave to a question of mine about the spiritual development of other species in their world, which was that, 'They also try to understand more.'

Throughout recorded history we have undoubtedly seen a definite progression in the communications claiming to originate from the next world. Such progression involves not only the shape of the contacts but also very markedly their quality. Through mental mediumship, one of the previous most important ways of transmission of information from another dimension, the main target seemed to be the proper identification of deceased personalities. In the new development attained through ITC phenomena, it is noticeable that the main purpose of the communicators seems to be to spread ethical guidance and transcendental information for the benefit of all. We have been the recipients of comprehensive contacts comprising long dialogues, outstanding images and computer texts of mind-boggling content. Furthermore, in just a few years – for instance during the time of my own experimentation – advanced ITC contacts seem to have spread exponentially to the point where DRV contacts, which were extremely rare until a few years ago, have become almost 'normal' happenings for ITC experimenters (see the *ITC Journal* Testimony Section).

Such rapid development raises the possibility that contacts with an unknown dimension of reality may become a fact of daily life for all who choose to involve themselves in ITC research. This would confirm the accuracy of Friedrich Jürgenson's prediction of the likelihood of a 'Telephone to the Beyond' in the near future. The other great pioneer of the ITC discipline, the late Konstantin Raudive, reportedly said in a communication to the Luxembourg group, when the new GA 1 system, which allowed for dialogues not previously feasible, was inaugurated: 'Here Konstantin Raudive, soon it will be possible everywhere!'

Certainly ITC contacts are a dynamic process but, at least consciously, we do not yet have the key to this process. While I write these lines, at the very beginning of the year 2009, there is currently a halt (hopefully temporary) in the communications received by many ITC experimenters. What does this imply? Only the future can tell. We humans live under finite conditions that most of us cannot see beyond, and any conjecture might therefore be dangerous because incorrect. In a perceptive, subjective way, my invisible communicators tell me that, 'We are researching ways to be able to speak directly to everybody interested in our [i.e. in their] world.' I still turn on my radios at the communicators' request quite frequently, but presently their voices cannot be heard in my house. However, I should also point out here that the communicators had promised me, through subjective perception, that they would try to imprint their messages during the series of tests that I am presently carrying out in the course of two major research projects on EVP voices. So far, the experiments have taken place in professional recording studios, acoustically shielded to the highest possible level, and in a semi-anechoic laboratory of the Department of Telecommunications of Vigo University, in Spain. Anomalous voices with very distinct characteristics have been recorded in virtually all the experiments despite the fact that we have used different methodologies, different equipment and different operators in each case. The work continues and hopefully very interesting findings and conclusions will be achieved. But these fascinating experiments fall outside the scope of this book, and I will report the results when the experiments have been concluded. Nevertheless, I would like to take this early opportunity to express my gratitude to the medical research foundation (which prefers for the present to remain anonymous) and to the Chair for the Study of Consciousness, Saybrook Graduate School and Research Center, San Francisco, California, USA, for their vision and for the confidence they have shown in my work. I sincerely hope that the results of the work will not disappoint them.

As early as February 2, 1909, exactly one century ago today, the late Frederic Myers purportedly said through Mrs. Willet's mediumship: 'The very active branch of our work this side is the experimental branch,' (Balfour, 1935). When requested to comment on the future of his research, Hans Otto König replied: 'I have no specific plans for the future because the development of the communication process depends, as I have said, essentially upon the communicators,' (Cardoso and Fernández, 2006). Based upon my personal experience, I fully endorse Hans Otto's opinion.

However, I can certainly speculate on the reasons that have

prompted the present silence of our communicators, although these must remain pure speculation (rest assured that even in the absence of new results, we already have an impressive amount of material on audio tapes and other electronic media to allow the scientific analysis that we seek to take place). Firstly, it is possible that I perceived correctly their subjective information, which informed me that it is related to the current stage of their research. Secondly, it may have to do with 'the permission to speak' which they require from higher entities and which, as they have repeatedly told us, is indispensable. Thirdly, it is possible that these high entities that apparently supervise ITC contacts find that the overwhelming downpour of information offered to humans since the middle of the 20th century has failed to prompt any noticeable changes in human consciousness at large. Or it could be due to a combination of these factors plus others that are still unknown. We should keep in mind that when questioned about the conditions that favor the contacts, the communicators replied noncommittally to the Luxembourg group: 'So many factors intervene in the contacts!' Rio do Tempo replied to my specific question on, 'Why are your communications sometimes so clear, other times not clear and still other times nonexistent?' with 'We don't know.' Perhaps it is all related to interdimensional quantum events.

Moreover, in an unconscious way, all of us without distinction might be responsible of influencing the trend of transcommunication. The admirable Antoine de Saint-Exupéry in 'The Little Prince' used the character of the fox to reveal an important secret. 'Il est très simple: On ne voit bien qu'avec le cœur. L'essentiel est invisible pour les yeux.' (It's quite simple: one sees clearly only with the heart. Anything essential is invisible to the eyes.) Outside time and space, in the boundless, uniting sea where the essence of all things, of all shapes or appearances, meet, we might be able to convey to our partners what our heart really wants. In this invisible, overwhelming sea of which we are not conscious, all things may become possible. The clearest of all EVP voices that I have recorded said, as I mentioned in previous chapters, '…they cannot hear me. **It has to be through the sea**.' In this infinite sea from where we all originate and to which we all belong, our original, true self might be able to speak. As an invisible and certainly wise communicator put it at Marcello Bacci's Center in Grosseto, on one of the occasions when I was present, 'What does your heart tell you?' Maybe our communicators will proceed from there, from what our heart tells them. An intriguing feminine voice from Rio do Tempo said about their world, 'Survival departure aqui'. ([Survival begins] here.) I believe that we need to wait and ultimately trust life.

Postscript

Latest Developments: 'Voltamos!'

When I received the manuscript of this book for proofreading, at the end of September 2009, wonderful developments had occurred in my studio a few weeks previously. Had I been requested to revise the proofs a little earlier, I would not have been able to announce the news of these developments to my readers now: Rio do Tempo voices can again be heard in my house on a regular basis!

It was the night of August 2nd, past midnight, and thus already the 3rd of August. My radios had been on since around 8.30pm because, with Rio do Tempo's agreement, by the middle of June I had gone back to experimenting with EVP regularly, as I had done at the beginning of my research in late 1997. I restarted the practice of EVP experimentation happily but, although I got some results, the voices were faint, and scarcely audible to an untrained ear.

I resumed EVP experiments on Thursdays and Sundays.

Before that, my radios were regularly on and off at the request of the communicators, as I explain elsewhere in the book, but no Direct Radio Voices were produced. For the last almost two years, I scrupulously fulfilled the routine of turning the radios on and off whenever Rio do Tempo mentally asked me to do so, and of being in the studio when they requested it but, to my great sorrow and disappointment, no voices could be heard during that long period that seemed forever to me.

During the last months of 2007, interesting things could sometimes be heard intermingled in Rio do Tempo's interminable recitation of the words that made up their 'work'. They said for instance, 'é a voz de outro tempo' (it is the voice of another time), and on another occasion, a well formed, well structured masculine voice replied to my insistent questions as to who was speaking with 'é teu pai' (it is your father) and it continued 'somos tio' (we are uncle), 'teu avô' (your grandfather), 'todos Cardoso' (all Cardoso) followed by the usual recitation of words. However, there was no consistent, direct conversation between the voices and me as it used to happen with Carlos de Almeida and even after he stopped communicating. It was as if laborious, hard work of training and research for the best ways to talk was going on somewhere in an invisible, unknown and mysterious dimension.

I would like to introduce here what, in my opinion, is the reason behind the expression 'todos Cardoso'. Cardoso is my surname from my father's side. My surname from my mother's and my dear grandmother's side (I assume it was my mother's mother who spoke with me on several occasions) is Mourato. My father had two brothers but I also have an uncle, my mother's brother, who was, naturally, Mourato. For several reasons, I was always closer to my mother's than to my father's family. I practically lived my childhood years with my maternal grandparents. When my father's father died I was very small, and the same thing happened with his mother who died just a few years later. I never really knew them, except for my father's description of them. My paternal grandfather, whom my father dearly loved and admired, must have been a remarkable man. The old type of gentleman, he was a man of character, a man of great honour and principles. But he was also an open minded man. A Freemason, he fought injustice at all cost and pursued the ideals of freedom and equality for all under the severe regime of Salazar, an enterprise that took him to jail and exile and put his life and his family's subsistence at stake (see Ventura, 2007). The voice says 'all Cardoso' and herewith clarifies the situation. Had it not been so, I would have naturally assumed that my 'grandfather' would be my mother's father whom I very much love, and who died when I was already an adult woman. Interestingly, years ago at the beginning of the DRV, a masculine voice once replied to my request of identification with 'o outro avô' (the other grand-father). My 'Cardoso' grandfather was not only an idealist but also a fighter who never gave up in the defense of his ideals and in his struggle for the destitute and for all who needed protection. A great lover of animals, also, it seems to me that he possessed the inner qualities that would drive him to get involved in the almost impossible task of helping in the construction of the bridge between this and the next dimension of life.

Although I did not give up all this time since 2007 and before, when the voices started to fail, it is true that I felt an inner pain difficult to describe and a great fatigue, often wondering what it was all about and why I was making all this effort. Nevertheless, I admit that the answer to this question, which I still ask myself now and then, is always – profound love for the communicators in general – for my father, my brother, my dear grandmother, my grandparents, my mother who died at a later stage of my ITC research, in 2003, and so far has not spoken with me, for my treasured Doberman dogs, who through their love and their demonstrations of lucidity opened unsuspected doors to me, for all the other abandoned animals that I sheltered, treated and learned to love, for all the many dear friends who are no longer with us but who once played such an important role in my life, for other animals and people who I briefly encountered long ago but remember with tenderness, for all departed family members that I never met, and for all the unknown communicators behind the enigmatic voices that could be heard so frequently in my house for so many years. I do not like to repeat phrases which, in my opinion, have lost all meaning and have become empty on account of the overuse and even abuse they have been subjected to, phrases such as, 'love is the reason behind all things', 'we are here [in this world] to learn and love', 'God is love', 'love is all there is', etc. Not only do I think that 'God is greater than love,' as Myers insisted in the work cited earlier, but for me God is equivalent to the life principle, to infinity, it is the invisible source. Also, at the human level (which is the only one we experience for now), I believe we cannot know true, complete love, an attribute that in its cosmic perspective must exceed our most ambitious vision. Yet, I can affirm without any doubt that, although in our humble, limited human way, love for the communicators was indeed the main force that moved me from the very beginning and has sustained me to this date throughout all efforts and sacrifices.

In the meantime, Rio do Tempo continued to tell me telepathically, 'We will be able to speak directly,' every time I conveyed my distress to them. But telepathic impressions are one thing, and clear, loud, mysterious voices that say they come from another world are a totally different thing; nothing surpasses the trust they inspire. Gloomy thoughts arising from some parapsychologists' and other supposedly well-informed experts' statements started coming to my mind, saddening me and disturbing me immensely. Statements such as, 'Anomalous phenomena are elusive and can suddenly be discontinued without any apparent cause;' 'It seems that God does not want us to cross a certain threshold of knowledge', etc. To my despair, I even thought that this might indeed be so in the case of Rio do Tempo and of their magnificent communications that had changed my life so dramatically. I felt miserable.

Then, on that night of August 2nd, 2009 with the moon waxing and the weather hot, the 'miracle' happened again and I rejoiced. There they were, Rio do Tempo Direct Radio Voices again! They have not stopped since then and often when I turn my radios on, following a regular schedule as I do now, the strange voices that I so much love can again be heard in my studio.

On the memorable night of last August 2, besides the usual feminine voices so typical of Rio do Tempo's communications, which seem to belong to what we might call announcers at the Station, a masculine voice speaking slowly, apparently with great effort although intelligibly, almost articulating every syllable one by one, replied to my request for identification: 'É Simão (a name I cannot recall as a close acquaintance); ... é teu irmão; morto; vivo.' (It is Simon; ... it is your brother; dead; alive.) And kept repeating other words of similar content (albeit some of which were not unquestionably understandable). The voices frequently said, 'morto; vivo' with the same monotonous cadence in the repetitions as was apparent in previous years but now directly replying to my questions. This magnificent, novel communication finished with the wonderful information: 'Teu perro vive (see use of the word 'perro' for dog on page 197); ...É a tua mãe; somos todos; Surya; puppy; vivem; ... este é o Cardoso.' (...Your dog lives; It is your mother; it is all of us; Surya [my beloved Doberman dog]; puppy; live; ... this is Cardoso.) The last words, 'este é o Cardoso,' were articulated in a slightly faster, more natural tone and are completely understandable to anybody, even those who have had no previous contact with electronic voices.

I will explain briefly the amazing implications of the reference to 'puppy'. My Doberman puppies were born in Tokyo, when I was posted to the Embassy in Japan. My faithful domestic helper, Ram Prasad Godyal, who worked at my house for ten years, was Indian and accompanied me to Japan when I was transferred to my new diplomatic posting. He had raised Surya and Nisha since they were little puppies in New Delhi. In Tokyo, by accident, Nisha had several puppies. Ram Prasad only spoke with me in English, and we kept to the habit of calling Surya's and Nisha's babies 'puppies', even years later in Portugal, where he accompanied me, when the four of them that remained with me had become adult dogs. Ram never managed to speak any Portuguese, so the new four Doberman dogs were 'puppies' for the rest of his stay in my house. My brother Luís did not know of this. Ram Prasad died a few years ago when I was posted as Consul General in Lyon, in France. I find it extremely impressive that the voice chose the word 'puppy' to refer to the rest of my beloved Doberman dogs. This was an expression known only by Ram Prasad, myself and the dogs.

I think we should also ponder the fact that the anomalous voice does not speak of Nisha, who had already directly spoken with me by DRV, as I mentioned in an earlier chapter. The economy of words is remarkable in this communication – besides using 'puppy' in the singular, the voice also says, 'morto; vivo,' (dead; alive) without further explanation. The verbs are missing but they are not necessary to convey the meaning. It reminds me, once again, that the process of communication must be a tremendously difficult task for the communicators. I have no doubt whatsoever about it and this is one of the rare points in ITC research that I have no doubts about!

There were other communications in August and September 2009, some of them very interesting such as the one when a very low masculine voice says: 'Não tem passagem.' (There is no passage.) And I say, 'This [the amplitude] is not enough for me to understand what you are saying.' Then, a feminine voice comes in and says 'A gente dá passagem' (We give passage), and the masculine voices become louder and more understandable.

On one of these occasions, when I asked about my grandmother, a masculine voice replied very pertinently and articulately, 'Estamos aqui com a tua avó, co's teus avós, estão todos aqui connosco.' (We are here with your grandmother, with your grandparents, they are all here with us.)

On September 25, Friday, a very moving contact took place. I only turned the radios on past midnight instead of doing it at the normal time, around 8.30 pm, on Thursday. The voices spoke at 9.15 pm, when I came back from the beach. This time the communicator spoke fluently and started with a glorious, 'Voltamos!' (We come back!). Undoubtedly, the voice sounded much more fluid and natural. It was a well-formed, soft masculine voice that announced twice in a happy, almost proud tone 'Voltamos!' and continued with the identification of the communicators as the dead, as '[Rio do] Tempo', and of the Station 'Esta é a Estação.' (This is the Station).

With a few exceptions, DRVs do not normally convey noticeable emotions. There was of course Carlos de Almeida who spoke with great fluidity, certainly expressing feelings, and giving the impression of an experienced, highly skilful communicator. But the majority of the voices, since he stopped communicating, express themselves with what sounds like a tremendous effort. Exceptions to this do happen however, as when a voice that identified itself as my father's, yelled in despair, 'É teu pai!' (It is your father!), in order to reply to my insistent question as to who was speaking; or when a soft voice (that I attributed to my maternal grandmother) said tenderly, 'Belinha [my pet name], já não sabes falar comigo?' (Belinha, can't you speak with me any longer?).

'Voltamos!', uttered with joy and serenity, sounded also victoriously. It was a delight to hear, and to know that Rio do Tempo had said, 'Voltamos!' filled my heart with tremendous love and gratitude. Tears keep falling from my eyes every time I listen to the recording of this communication.

'Valeu tudo a pena!' (Everything was worth it!), said my father years ago, through ITC, when I asked him if all the sacrifices he had gone through in this life had been worth it from the perspective of his new life. Likewise, on September 25, 2009, Rio do Tempo said 'Voltamos!' and suddenly everything was indeed worth it.

Endnotes

1 For a good description and explanation of the term white noise – which is normally used inaccurately in ITC literature – see Philip Newell's *Terminological inexactitudes*, published in *ITC Journal* 33, 2008.

2 The technical details were kindly confirmed by electro-acoustics engineer Philip Newell who, at the time, worked at Pye Records with the now deceased Ken Attwood.

3 Information conveyed to Philip Newell in 2008 by Ray Prickett who currently lives near London.

4 According to Ray Prickett, the device he monitored was an *oscilloscope*.

5 Information conveyed to Philip Newell by Ray Prickett.

6 The method of the diode consists of an elementary radio that incorporates a diode which is used as a detector, or demodulator of the carrier for the revelation of the voices.

References

Alcântara, L. (2008). Testimony – significant sequence. *ITC Journal*, 31, pp. 66–68.

Alcântara, L. (2008). Significant elements of my ITC experimentation. *ITC Journal*, 31, pp 64–66.

Alvisi, G. (1976). *As Vozes dos Vivos de Ontem*. Mem Martins, Portugal: Publicações Europa-América.

Alvisi, G. (1983). *Dimensione Radiosa*. Milano: SugarCo. Edizioni s.r.l.

Andrade, H. G. (1997). *A Transcomunicacão Através dos Tempos*. São Paulo: Editora Jornalistica FE.

Bacci, M. (1991). *Il Mistero delle Voci dall' Aldillà*. 2nd ed. Roma: Ed. Mediterranee.

Balfour, G. (1935). 'A study of the psychological aspects of Mrs. Willet's mediumship, and of the statements of the communicators concerning process'. *Proceedings of the SPR*, Part 140, Vol. 43, p. 159.

Bander, P. (1972). *Carry on Talking*. Gerrards Cross, UK: Colin Smythe.

Bander, P. (1973). *Voices from the Tapes*. New York: Drake Publishers Inc.

Bender, H. (1970). Zur Analyse aussergewöhnlicher Stimmphänomene auf Tonband. Erkundungsexperimente über dir « Einspielungen » von Friedrich Jürgenson. *ZSPP (Zeitschrift für Parapsychologie und Grenzgebiete der Psychologie)*, 12, 226-238, Freiburg i. Br: Walter-Verlag.

Bender, H. (1976). *Verborgene Wirklichkeit*. Munich: Deutscher Taschenbuch Verlag.

Bose, J. (1902). Response in the Living and Non-Living. New York: Longmans Green.

Bose, J. (1913). Researches on Irritability of Plants. New York: Longmans Green.

Bose, J. (1926). The Nervous Mechanism of Plants. New York: Longmans Green.

Bozzano, E. (1941). *Popoli Primitivi e manifestazioni supernormali*. Verona: Edizioni L'Albero.

Britten, Emma H. (1870). *Modern American Spiritualism*. New York: the Author.

Brune, F. (1993). *Les Morts nous Parlent*. Paris: Ed. du Félin, Philippe Lebaud (1st ed. 1988).

Brune, F. (2005, 2006). *Les Morts nous Parlent*. (3rd. Ed.) Tome 1 (2005), Tome 2 (2006). Paris: Oxus Editions.

Brune, F. and Chauvin, R. (2003). *À L'Écoute de L'Au-Delà*. 2nd. Ed. Paris: Oxus.

Cardoso, A. (2003). Survival research. *Journal of Conscientiology*. Vol. 6, nº 21, pp. 33-63.

Cardoso, A. (2005). Translation of the transcript from the two original recordings made by Marcello Bacci and Anabela Cardoso at Grosseto on 5 December 2004. *ITC Journal* 21, pp. 25-33.

Cardoso, A. (2005). ITC: personal results and guidance on methodology. In Cardoso, A. and Fontana, D. (Eds.). *Proceedings of the First International Conference on Current Research into Survival of Physical Death with Special Reference to Instrumental Transcommunication*. Vigo, Spain: ITC Journal Publications.

Cardoso, A. (2006). Marcello Bacci interviewed by Anabela Cardoso. *ITC Journal*, 25, pp. 19-22.

Cardoso, A. (2007). Instrumental Transcommunication – Contact with another reality potentially open to all. *Proceedings of the Second International Conference on Current Research into Survival of Physical Death with Special Reference to Instrumental Transcommunication*. York, England: Saturday Night Press Publications for ITC Journal Research Center, Vigo, Spain.

Cardoso, A. (2007). The Overwhelming Spread of Instrumental Transcommunication Contacts of High Quality. *ITC Journal*,

28, pp. 3-6.

Cardoso, A. and Fernández, C. (2006). Thought is a force that creates and destroys worlds, an interview with Hans Otto König. *ITC Journal*, 27, pp. 37-41.

Cardoso, A. and Fontana, D. (eds.) (2005). *Proceedings of the First International Conference on Current Research into Survival of Physical Death with Special Reference to Instrumental Transcommunication (ITC)*. Vigo, Spain: ITC Journal Publications.

Carrington, H. (1907). *The Physical Phenomena of Spiritualism*. Boston: Small, Maynard & Co.

Cummins, G. (1932). *The Road to Immortality*. London: Ivor Nicholson & Watson.

D'Argonnel, O. (1925). *Vozes do Além pelo Telefone*. Rio de Janeiro: Pap. Typ. Marques, Araújo & C.

David-Neel, A. (1967). *Magic and Mystery in Tibet*. London: Souvenir Press (re-published in Corgi Books 1971).

Estep, S. (1988). *Voices of Eternity*. New York: Fawcett Gold Medal Book, Ballantine Books.

Estep, S. (2005). *Roads to Eternity*, Galde Press, Inc. PO Box 460 Lakeville MN 55044, USA.

Fernández, C. (2006). *Voces del Más Allá. ¿Hablan los Fallecidos a través de los Equipos Electrónicos?* Madrid: Editorial Edaf S. A. (El Archivo del Misterio de Iker Jiménez)

Festa, M. (2002). A particular experiment at the psychoponic center in Grosseto, directed by Marcello Bacci. *ITC Journal*, 10, pages 27-31.

Fisher, J. (1990). *Hungry Ghosts*. London: Grafton Books.

Fodor, N. (1974). *Encyclopaedia of Psychic Science*. Secaucus, New Jersey: The Citadel Press.

Fontana, D. and Cardoso, A. (2002). Developing a protocol for DVR. *ITC Journal*, 12, pages 55-57.

Fontana, D. (2003). Le ricerche sull T.C.S., con particolare riferimento al l'opera di Anabela Cardoso. *La Richerca Psichica* X, 3,

77-92.

Fontana, D. (2005). *Is There an Afterlife?* Ropley, Hants, UK: John Hunt/O Books.

Fornoff, J. (2009). My journey to the discovery of ABX Juno. *ITC Journal*, 34, pp. 90-92; *ITC Journal*, 35, pp. 60-68.

Fukuoka, M. (1987). *The Road back to Nature.* Tokyo, New York: Japan Publications, Inc.

Fuller, J. G. (1985). *The Ghost of 29 Megacycles.* London: Souvenir Press Ltd.

Gettings, F. (1986). *Encyclopaedia of the Occult.* London: Rider & Co.

Grandsire, J. M. (1998). *La Transcommunication.* Agnières: JMG editions.

Gullà, D. (2005). Computer-Based Analysis of Supposed Paranormal Voices: The Question of Anomalies Detected and Speaker Identification. In A. Cardoso and D. Fontana (eds.) *Proceedings of the First International Conference on Current Research into Survival of Physical Death with Special Reference to Instrumental Transcommunication (ITC).* Vigo, Spain: ITC Journal Publications.

Gullà, D. (2007). Voice signal enhancement: processing and post-processing. In A. Cardoso and D. Fontana (eds.) *Proceedings of the Second International Conference on Current Research into Survival of Physical Death with Special Reference to Instrumental Transcommunication (ITC).* Vigo, Spain: ITC Journal Publications.

Holbe, R. (1987). *Bilder aus dem Reich der Toten.* Munich: Droemersche Verlogsanstalt Th. Knaur Nachf.

Holbe, R. (1989). *Immagini dal Regno dei Morti.* Roma: Edizioni Mediterranee.

Jacobson, N. O. (1973). *Life without Death?* New York: Delacorte/Seymour Lawrence.

Jürgenson, F. (1964). *Röstema från Rymden* (Voices from the Space).

Stockholm: Saxon & Lindströms.

Jürgenson, F. (1967). *Sprechfunk mit Verstorbenen* (Freiburg im Br.: Verlag Hermann Bauer. Republished 1981 by Goldmann Verlag (München).

Jürgenson, F. (1968). *Radio och Mikrofonkontakt med de döda*. (Radio and microphone contacts with the dead) Uppsala: Nybloms.

Jürgenson, F. (2004). *Voice Transmissions with the Deceased.* Stockholm: Firework Edition Nº 101. The Jürgenson Foundation: http://www.fargfabriken.se/fjf/

Kardec, Allan (1857). *Le Livre des Esprits*. Paris: Dentu.

Kardec, A. (1864). *Revue Spirite.*

König, H. (2007). Psychic structures as connections to other realities. In A. Cardoso and D. Fontana (eds.) *Proceedings of the Second International Conference on Current Research into Survival of Physical Death with Special Reference to Instrumental Transcommunication (ITC).* York, England: Saturday Night Press Publications on behalf of ITC Journal Research Center, Vigo, Spain.

Laszlo, E. (2008). *Quantum Shift in the Global Brain*. Vermont, USA: Inner Traditions.

Laszlo, E. (2008). An Unexplored Domain of Nonlocality: Toward a Scientific Explanation of Instrumental Transcommunication. *Explore,* September/October, Vol. 4, Nº 5, 321-327.

Locher, T. and Harsch, M. (1989). *Les Contacts vers l'Au-delà à l'aide de moyens techniques existent !* Association Suisse de Parapsychologie et Cercle d'Etudes sur la Transcommunication du Luxembourg. (1995, French ed. Agnières: Parasciences).

MacRae, A. (1984). Some findings relative to the electronic voice phenomenon. (Mark 1, PSI Research March issue, page 36-46).

Meek, G. (1987). *After We die, What Then?* Atlanta, USA: Ariel Press.

Pearson, K. A. and Mullarkey, J. (eds.). (2002). *Key Writings of Henri Bergson*. London: Continuum.

Pilón, J. M. (1996). *Lo paranormal ¿existe?* Madrid: Ediciones Temas de Hoy.

Presi, P. (1990). Psicofonia e paranormalità elettroniche. *Esperienze Paranormali*, Edizioni Mediterranee.

Presi, P. (2009). A pioneer in EVP research: Dr. Renato Orso from Turin. *ITC Journal.* 35, pp.28-39.

Radin, D. (2006). *Entangled Minds.* New York: Simon & Schuster, Inc. (Pocket Books).

Raudive, K. (1968). *Unhörbares Wird Hörbar – Auf den Spuren Einer Geisterwelt.* Remagen: Reichl.

Raudive, K. (1971). *Breakthrough: An Amazing Experiment in Electronic Communication with the Dead.* Gerrards Cross, England: Colin Smythe.

Schäfer, H. (1989). *Brücke Zwischen Diesseits und Jenseits.* Freiburg: Verlag Hermann Bauer KG.

Schäfer, H. (1993). *Ponte entre o Aqui e o Além - Teoria e Prática da Transcomunicação.* São Paulo, Editora Pensamento (Portuguese translation of the above mentioned work).

Schmidt, H. (1970). PK experiments with animals as subjects. *Journal of Parapsychology*, Vol. 34, 4, December 1970, pp. 255-261.

Scott Rogo, D. and Bayless, R. (1979). *Phone Calls from the Dead.* Englewood Cliffs, New Jersey: Prentice-Hall.

Senkowski, E. (1995). *Instrumentelle Transkommunikation* (first ed. 1989) Frankfurt: R. G. Fischer.

Senkowski, E. (1999). Die Transkontakte des Adolf Homes - Ein rückblick. Teil 1: übersicht und transpartner (The transcontacts of Adolf Homes - A review. Part 1: Synopsis and Transpartners). *TransKommunikation.* Vol. IV, No.1, pp. 12-31.

Sheldrake, R. (1999). *Dogs that Know When Their Owners are Coming Home.* London: Hutchinson.

Spence, L. (1974). *An Encyclopaedia of Occultism.* N. Jersey (USA): The Citadel Press.

Swedenborg, E. (1853). *Compendium of the Theological and Spiritual*

Writings of Emanuel Swedenborg. Boston: Crosby and Nichols, pp. 160-197.

Théry, P. (2000). First telephone contact in France by Konstantin Raudive. *ITC Journal*, 2, 42-43.

Trajna, C. (1983). Le voci dirette di Grosseto. *Il Giornale dei Misteri*, 149, 38-40.

Trajna, C. (1985). Introduction in Bacci's *Il Mistero Delle Voci Dall'Aldilà*. Roma: Edizioni Mediterranee.

Trajna, C. (2000-2001). The Psychotemporal Model. *ITC Journal* 1-7.

Ventura, A. (2007). *A Maçonaria no Distrito de Portalegre*. Casal de Cambra, Portugal: Caledoscópio, SA.

Winter, J. and Dampierre, G. (1939). Messages inédits. *Le Messager*, 61, 7-8.

BOOKS

O is a symbol of the world, of oneness and unity. In different cultures it also means the "eye," symbolizing knowledge and insight. We aim to publish books that are accessible, constructive and that challenge accepted opinion, both that of academia and the "moral majority."

Our books are available in all good English language bookstores worldwide. If you don't see the book on the shelves ask the bookstore to order it for you, quoting the ISBN number and title. Alternatively you can order online (all major online retail sites carry our titles) or contact the distributor in the relevant country, listed on the copyright page.

See our website **www.o-books.net** for a full list of over 500 titles, growing by 100 a year.

And tune in to myspiritradio.com for our book review radio show, hosted by June-Elleni Laine, where you can listen to the authors discussing their books.